Explore TIPS

A practical guide to investing in Treasury Inflation-Protected Securities

By

The Finance Buff

To Linda

Contents

Contents

Preface

This short book is all about TIPS – the inflation indexed bonds. I invest in TIPS because they provide unique inflation protection not found elsewhere.

The financial media write much more about stock investing than they do about bond investing. Many investors say they don't understand bonds. With the added complexity of inflation indexing, investing in TIPS can be even more confusing.

Mystery no more! In this book I will share with you all the details a retail investor would ever need to know about TIPS and how to invest in them. I will also share with you the tools I created to help you make decisions.

This is not a book on investment theory. Everything is meant to be practical. I go into details most other books gloss over. I write from a retail investor's perspective because I *am* a retail investor. I learned almost everything in this book from my own experience investing in TIPS.

No prior knowledge is required. Even if you know nothing about TIPS now, after you read this book, I hope you will be comfortable investing in TIPS.

Acknowledgement

I'd like to thank Austin Frakt and Mike Piper. This book would not be possible without them.

Austin and Mike were very generous to me with their time. They thoroughly reviewed a draft of this book. I can't thank them enough for their valuable feedback and encouragement.

Austin is an Assistant Professor and a health economist at Boston University. He writes a great blog at *TheIncidentalEconomist.com*.

Mike Piper is the author of several books, including *Investing Made Simple*, *Taxes Made Simple*, and *Oblivious Investing*. I read Mike's blog every day at *ObliviousInvestor.com*.

Explore TIPS

A practical guide to investing in Treasury Inflation-Protected Securities

Chapter 1 Bonds Refresher

Before we dive into TIPS, let's have a refresher for some basic bond concepts. These concepts apply to all bonds, including TIPS, but they are not specific to TIPS:

- How bonds are different from CDs
- Yield and discounting future value
- The relationship between price and yield
- A bond ladder and a bond mutual fund
- Bonds and taxes

If you are already familiar with bonds in general, you can skip this chapter and go directly to Chapter 2.

CDs Are Bonds Too

Most people are familiar with Certificates of Deposit (CDs). You can buy these at a bank. You give the bank a sum of money for a specified period of time. The bank pays you interest. When the term is up, you get your money back.

A CD is the simplest form of a bond. It has the basic elements of a bond. If you understand CDs, you already understand the simplest bonds.

Issuer. The issuer of a bond is the entity that borrows money from you. In a CD, the bank is the issuer.

Principal. The principal is the amount of money you lend to the issuer. By convention, bonds go by multiples of $1,000. 1 bond is $1,000 in principal.

Maturity. A bond's maturity is similar to the term of a CD. It can be expressed as a date or as the length of time until such date arrives. That date is the date when the issuer pays the principal back to you. If a bond's maturity is in the near future, usually five years or less, the bond is a *short-term bond*. If a bond's maturity date is way out in the future, usually 15 years or more, the bond is a *long-term bond*. If its maturity is between short-term and long-term, the bond is an *intermediate-term bond*.

Interest Rate. This is the interest rate that a bond's issuer will pay for borrowing money from you. It's expressed as an annual rate although bonds usually pay interest every six months. The interest rate is also called the *coupon rate* because in the old days investors would clip off a coupon from a paper bond and send it back to the issuer to collect interest payment.

Bonds Trade

If that's all there is to bonds, bond investing wouldn't be so confusing. A key difference between bonds and CDs is that bonds trade. Although some CDs also trade, most CDs don't: you buy a CD; the bank pays you interest periodically; when the term is up, you get your money back. That's the life of a CD.

With a bond, the owners can trade it with other investors in the market. The price at which a bond trades determines the value of your bond even if you don't trade yours. The bond market tells you how much your bond is worth based on the latest trade. You see the value of your bond go up and down. This is called *mark to market*.

With mark-to-market, even though your bond pays in full at maturity and you collect interest along the way, you may "lose money" in the interim when your bond's market value falls below its principal.

Present Value and Yield to Maturity

The bond market determines the value of your bond by calculating its *present value*. $1,000 in the future is worth less than $1,000 today because if you have $1,000 today you can earn interest on it and make it grow to more than $1,000 in the future. This concept is called *time value of money.*

The mechanism to get the present value of a sum of money in the future is called *discounting*. The math formula for discounting is:

$$Present\ Value = \frac{Future\ Value}{(1 + interest\ rate)^{number\ of\ years}}$$

For example, if interest rate is 6% a year, the present value of $1,000 five years from today is:

$$\frac{\$1,000}{(1 + 6\%)^5} = \$747.26$$

The present value of $20 six months from today is:

$$\frac{\$20}{(1 + 6\%)^{0.5}} = \$19.43$$

The present value of $20 one year from today is:

$$\frac{\$20}{(1 + 6\%)^1} = \$18.87$$

If a bond pays $1,000 five years from now, plus $20 in interest every six months, you will get the fair price of this bond after you add up the present value for the principal payback and for each interest payment.

Bond price = $747.26 + $19.43 + $18.87 + ...

On the other hand, if you know what the market price of a bond is, you can calculate the necessary interest rate that will make the sum of the present values equal to its market price. This interest rate is the bond's *yield to maturity* (YTM).

Suppose the bond's price is $894.46, you must solve the interest rate *i* in the following equation:

$$894.46 = \frac{1000}{(1+i)^5} + \frac{20}{(1+i)^{0.5}} + \frac{20}{(1+i)^1} + \ldots + \frac{20}{(1+i)^5}$$

Calculating a bond's yield to maturity by hand requires tedious trial-and-error. With the aid of a financial calculator or a computer, one can easily calculate a bond's YTM given a bond's price.

Price, Interest Rate, and Duration

The market price of a particular bond is affected by the prevailing interest rate relevant to that bond.

If your bond pays 4% interest when other similar bonds are paying 6%, other investors will not pay $1,000 for your $1,000 bond because they can get 6% elsewhere. They will pay less than $1,000 for your bond such that they will still earn 6% on the price they pay. On the other hand, if the best they can get elsewhere is 2%, they will be willing to pay a higher price for your 4% bond.

Therefore there exists an inverse relationship between a bond's price and the relevant prevailing interest rate. A bond's price goes down when interest rate goes up; a bond's price goes up when interest rate goes down. Remember this basic relationship between bond price and interest rate.

Please note I qualified prevailing interest rate with the word *relevant,* because there is not just one interest rate. There are short-term interest rates and there are long-term interest rates and they don't necessarily go up and down in parallel. If short-term interest rate goes up, long-term interest rate can go up, go down, or stay the same. If you have a short-term bond, its price is affected by the short-term interest rate. If you have a long-term bond, its price is affected by the long-term interest rate.

If you plot the bond maturities on the X axis with the corresponding interest rates on the Y axis, the resulting curve is called the *yield curve.* When the difference between short-term interest rate and long-term interest rate is high, it's a *steep* yield curve. When that difference is small, it's a *flat* yield curve. When short-term interest rate is higher than long-term interest rate, it's an *inverted* yield curve.

Figure 1 on the next page shows a steep yield curve and an inverted yield curve.

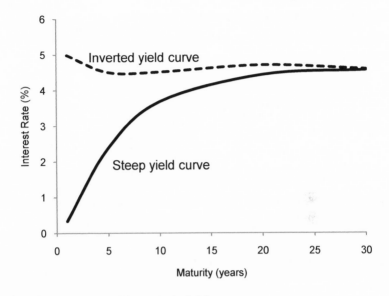

Figure 1: Steep and inverted yield curves

The bond's remaining life to maturity also affects the degree to which its price changes in response to interest rate changes. If the bond is close to its maturity, its price will change very little for each 1% change in short-term interest rate. If the bond has many years until maturity, its price will change much more for each 1% change in long-term interest rate.

The degree to which the bond's price would change for each 1% change in interest rate is the bond's *duration*. A bond's duration is expressed as a number of years. It can be calculated from the bond's current price, its coupon rate, and its maturity date. If a bond is said to have a duration of 7 years, it means the bond's price will go down by 7% if the relevant prevailing interest rate goes up by 1% tomorrow.

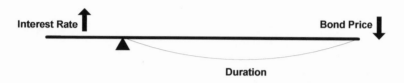

Figure 2: The inverse relationship between bond price and interest rate changes

Bond Ladder and Bond Funds

A bond *ladder* is a collection of bonds with maturities in approximate equal distance from one another. For instance if you have a three-year bond, a six-year bond, a nine-year bond and a 12-year bond, you have a bond ladder, with each rung three years apart. Of course you don't have to have the rungs three years apart. You can have a ladder from one year to ten years, with the rungs one year apart.

If you don't need money from the ladder, when one bond matures, you buy a new bond at the far end of the ladder. In the 3-, 6-, 9-, and 12-year bond ladder example, when the 3-year bond matures, the original 6-, 9-, and 12-year bonds now have 3, 6, and 9 years remaining respectively. You use the money from the matured bond to buy a new 12-year bond and restore your ladder.

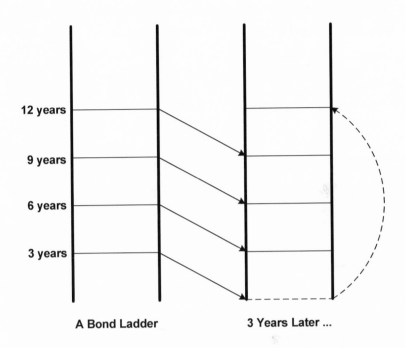

A Bond Ladder   **3 Years Later ...**

Figure 3: Restoring a bond ladder after a bond matures

If you need money from the ladder, for example when you are already retired and you use the money to supplement your income, you can just spend the money as each bond matures. The ladder naturally winds down itself. A self-destructing ladder is very popular among retirees because it provides predictable cash flow for retirement income.

A bond *fund* is a mutual fund that invests in bonds. An investment manager selects which bonds to buy, hold, and sell. The mutual fund investor owns a small piece of all the bonds in the fund. The investment manager is paid a percentage of the fund assets.

A bond fund can hold hundreds or even thousands of bonds. Buying that many bonds for a bond ladder is impractical for an individual investor except the very wealthy with millions of dollars to invest. For bonds other than U.S. Treasury and TIPS, buying many bonds through a bond fund also reduces risks through diversification.

Bonds and Taxes

The investment returns from bonds come primarily from the interest payments. Investors generally must pay taxes each year on the interest income unless the bonds are held in a tax deferred or a tax free (Roth) account.

If held in a taxable account, bonds issued by the U.S. Treasury are exempt from state and local income taxes.

A special category of bonds called municipal bonds are tax exempt. Municipal bonds are out of scope for this book.

Tax efficiency refers to the extent of an investment's return that can be retained by the investor after all taxes are paid. Because an investor must pay taxes every year on interest income at the highest marginal tax rate, bonds are said to be not tax efficient. As a result, in general bonds should be held in a tax deferred or a tax free account to minimize taxes.

There are special rules for taxes on TIPS. They are covered on page 30 in Chapter 2.

More on Bonds

That's all for a quick refresher on bonds, just enough prep work for the rest of this book. If you'd like to read more about bonds, I recommend these two books:

The Bond Book by Annette Thau. ISBN 978-0071358620. A new edition of this book is forthcoming in June 2010.

The Only Guide to a Winning Bond Strategy You'll Ever Need By Larry E. Swedroe and Joseph H. Hempen. ISBN 978-0312353636.

Chapter 2 TIPS Basics

Chapter 1 gives you a refresher on bonds in general. From this chapter forward, we focus exclusively on TIPS. First, let's explore the basics of investing in TIPS:

- What TIPS are and what makes them attractive
- How they compare to other investments
- Taxes and risks
- How to buy TIPS if you like them

What Are TIPS

TIPS are **T**reasury **I**nflation-**P**rotected **S**ecurities. They are a special kind of bond issued by the U.S. Treasury. TIPS are special because their principal and interest are indexed to grow with inflation.

A regular, or in bond-speak, *nominal* Treasury bond is an IOU. When the government borrows $100 from you, they promise to pay you back $100 sometime in the future. While they have your money, they pay you interest every six months. The interest payments are fixed. If you have a bond that pays 4% a year, for every $100 you lend to the government, you receive $2 interest every six months. At the end of the term of the bond, the government pays you back the $100 you lent to it.

TIPS work the same way, except everything is tied to the Consumer Price Index (CPI), which is a common measure of inflation. The government borrows $100 from you today. When they pay you back, if CPI doubled, they pay you back $200. That $200 in the future has the same purchasing power as $100 today. Your purchasing power is preserved.

The interest payments are also tied to CPI. If you receive $1.00 interest in year 1 and CPI increased by 50% by year 15, you will receive $1.50 interest in year 15. After adjusting for inflation, that $1.50 in year 15 has the same purchasing power as $1.00 in year 1.

Because the principal payback and the interest payments increase with inflation, TIPS are said to have inflation protection.

Like other Treasury bonds, TIPS are also guaranteed by the full faith and credit of the United States government. The interest you receive from TIPS is taxable under federal income tax, but exempt from state and local income tax.

Real vs. Nominal

The concepts of real and nominal are very important in understanding TIPS. I will use these two terms repeatedly throughout this book.

Real means after adjusting for inflation. $1.00 in 1979 has the same purchasing power as $2.98 in 2009.

That $2.98 value is a *nominal* value. In *real* terms, it's the same as $1.00 in 1979.

Bonds that pay interest and principal in nominal dollars are called *nominal bonds*. The vast majority of bonds are nominal bonds. Unless in the context of comparing to TIPS and other inflation indexed bonds, nominal bonds are just referred to as bonds.

TIPS and other inflation indexed bonds are called *real return bonds* because they provide a guaranteed inflation-adjusted return.

If someone invested $1.00 in 1979 and the investment grew to $2.98 in 2009, the nominal rate of return is 3.71%.

$$(1 + 3.71\%)^{30} = 2.98$$

But after adjusting for inflation, the real rate of return is exactly zero because the purchasing power of this investment did not increase at all.

When you are investing, you are investing for the future. For the future, only *real* dollars and *real* rate of return matter. Without a positive real rate of return, your investment is not gaining value even though the nominal rate of return is positive.

You can calculate the real rate of return from the nominal rate of return and inflation. The formula is:

$$real\ return\ =\ \frac{1 + nominal\ return}{1 + inflation} - 1$$

For example, when the nominal return is 5% a year and inflation is 3% a year, the real return is:

$$\frac{1 + 5\%}{1 + 3\%} - 1 = 1.94\%$$

When inflation isn't too high, the calculation can be approximated as:

$$real\ return\ =\ nominal\ return\ -\ inflation$$

If we use the approximation formula, when the nominal return is 5% a year and inflation is 3% a year, the real return is:

$$5\% - 3\% = 2\%$$

It's close to 1.94% number from the precise formula.

Why Buy TIPS?

Why should an investor buy TIPS? To make money, of course.

TIPS are bonds. Investors buy TIPS for all the reasons they buy bonds: for earning interest income; for lowering risk in their investment portfolio; and for speculating on interest rate changes.

TIPS are issued by the United States Treasury. Investors buy TIPS for the same reason they buy Treasury bonds: for their high credit quality. The interest payment and principal repayment are guaranteed by the full faith and credit of the United States government.

Most importantly, investors buy TIPS for inflation protection. Because the principal repayment and the interest payments are indexed to inflation, TIPS offer guaranteed inflation protection.

No matter how high inflation goes after you buy TIPS, you know for sure your interest income and your final principal payback will go up at the same pace as inflation as measured by the Consumer Price Index. Nominal bonds don't have this guarantee.

The interest payments and the principal payback on nominal bonds are fixed. The biggest enemy to nominal bonds is inflation. Over time, inflation eats away the value of the interest and the principal.

A bond with a 5% interest rate sounds good if inflation is 2% a year, but it's not so good if inflation is 8% a year. With TIPS, you are guaranteed a real interest rate after inflation, regardless whether inflation ends up being 2% or 8%.

Therefore buying TIPS is like buying insurance on unexpected inflation. An investor concerned about the impact of higher than expected inflation should consider buying TIPS as a part of a balanced portfolio.

TIPS vs. Nominal Bonds

Do nominal bonds also protect you from inflation? Yes and no. Nominal bonds offer protection for expected inflation, while TIPS offer protection for unexpected inflation.

Because some level of inflation is expected, the inflation protection in TIPS does not come free. The stated *real* interest rate on TIPS is typically lower than the stated *nominal* interest rate on nominal bonds of the same maturity.

For example in December 2009, the real interest rate on 10-year TIPS was about 1.3%, while the interest rate on 10-year nominal Treasury was about 3.5%. If the Consumer Price Index increases by 2.2% a year in each of the following ten years, an investor will receive the same return from either the 10-year TIPS or the 10-year nominal Treasury. If inflation increases by more than 2.2% a year, an investor will be better off investing in the 10-year TIPS. If inflation increases by less than 2.2% a year, an investor will be better off investing in the 10-year nominal Treasury.

As long as the interest rate on a nominal bond is higher than inflation, the interest will make up for inflation's erosion on the principal. Your money's purchasing power is preserved.

If inflation becomes higher than expected and it exceeds the fixed interest rate on a nominal bond, you will not be able to preserve the purchasing power with the nominal bond.

The nominal investment return on TIPS comes from the real interest rate and the inflation adjustment. If inflation comes in lower than expected, the nominal return from TIPS will be lower as well. In such case, all else being equal, nominal bonds will do better than TIPS. However, if inflation is higher than expected, nominal bonds will do worse than TIPS. For this reason, TIPS are said to offer protection for unexpected inflation, while nominal bonds offer protection for expected inflation. Nominal bonds also offer better protection for deflation.

Table 1 on the next page shows the cash flows of a nominal 10-year Treasury bond with a 5% interest rate and the cash flows of a 10-year TIPS with a 2% interest rate, when inflation is 3% per year over 10 years. A negative number represents cash outflow, i.e. money going out of your pocket, while a positive number represents cash inflow, i.e. money coming into your pocket.

Table 1 Hypothetical Cash Flows

Year	In Nominal Dollars		In Real Dollars	
	Nominal Bond	TIPS	Nominal Bond	TIPS
0	-1,000.00	-1,000.00	-1,000.00	-1,000.00
1	50.00	20.45	48.91	20.00
2	50.00	21.06	47.48	20.00
3	50.00	21.69	46.10	20.00
4	50.00	22.35	44.76	20.00
5	50.00	23.02	43.45	20.00
6	50.00	23.71	42.19	20.00
7	50.00	24.42	40.96	20.00
8	50.00	25.15	39.76	20.00
9	50.00	25.90	38.61	20.00
10	1,050.00	1,370.60	781.58	1,020.00
Rate of Return	5%	5%	2%	2%

In this hypothetical example the nominal bond and the TIPS bond have the same investment return but the cash flows are different.

The nominal bond pays more interest, steady in nominal dollars, but declining in real dollars. The nominal bond's final payoff value is lower because part of the return is already paid out via higher interest payments.

The TIPS bond pays lower interest, increasing in nominal dollars, but steady in real dollars. The final payout is higher because there is no erosion to the principal's purchasing power.

Effectively, part of the interest from the TIPS bond is automatically reinvested and postponed until the bond matures. If part of the interest from the nominal bond is also reinvested, the cash flows will be similar.

However, the rates of return on these two bonds will be different if the inflation rate is not 3%. Figure 4 on the next page shows the nominal returns under different inflation rates.

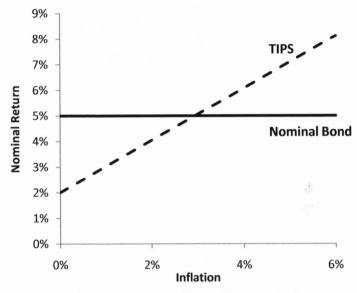

Figure 4: Nominal Returns Under Different Inflation

In terms of nominal returns, the nominal bond's return remains the same while the TIPS' return goes up with higher inflation. Figure 5 on the next page shows the real returns under different inflation rates.

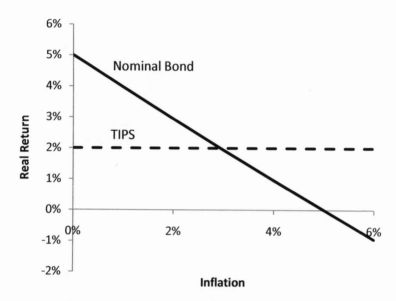

Figure 5: Real Returns Under Different Inflation

The nominal bond's real return declines with higher inflation while the TIPS' real return remains the same.

TIPS vs. I Bonds

Series I Savings Bonds ("I Bonds") are another type of inflation indexed bond issued by the U.S. Treasury. Both TIPS and I Bonds offer inflation protection.

How are they different? In a nutshell, TIPS work like a bond, while I Bonds work like a CD.

Like all bonds, TIPS are traded on the secondary market after they are issued. Every day, the buyers and sellers on the market determine the price and yield of each TIPS bond, which will be different from the price and yield when the bond was originally issued.

TIPS prices fluctuate, both up and down, depending on the market. However, because there is an active market, the price and yield are considered to be fair at any time.

I Bonds on the other hand don't trade on the secondary market. They earn a variable interest rate. Their values only go up or stay the same, but never go down.

Every six months, the Treasury Department announces the base rate for new I Bonds and inflation adjustment for all I Bonds.

If the base rate on newer I Bonds goes down, your existing I Bonds don't get a boost in principal value like TIPS would when market interest rate goes down. Your older I Bonds only earn a higher interest rate than the newer I Bonds.

If you have those high-base-rate I Bonds, the best you can do is hold them until they mature. You can't sell your high-rate I Bonds for a higher price to someone else as you would with TIPS. Essentially you lose liquidity from your older, better I Bonds.

On the other hand, if the base interest rate on newer I Bonds goes up, you can redeem your lower rate I Bonds without suffering a loss like you would from TIPS when market interest rate goes up.

This feature on I Bonds is a *put option*. Because of this built-in put option, and because the base rate on I Bonds is set arbitrarily by the issuer — the U.S. Treasury — the interest rate on I Bonds can be a lot lower than the interest rate on TIPS set by the market.

The yield on I Bonds can't be considered as fair. I Bonds purchasers often pay dearly for the no-loss guarantee.

I Bonds are easier to buy in smaller quantities; the lowest I Bonds purchase starts at $25. For large purchases though, U.S. Treasury limits I Bonds purchases to $10,000 per social security number per year: $5,000 maximum electronically, plus another $5,000 maximum in paper. With TIPS, investors can buy practically as much as they want.

TIPS can be bought in an IRA. I Bonds can only be bought with taxable money, although I Bonds themselves are tax deferred.

If I Bonds are used for education purpose and the purchaser meets some other conditions including an income level qualification, the interest is tax free. There is no such feature on TIPS.

Table 2 on the next page summarizes the major differences between TIPS and I Bonds.

Table 2 Major difference between TIPS and I Bonds

	TIPS	I Bonds
Interest rate set by	Market	U.S. Treasury
Price fluctuation	Fluctuates	Can't go down
Liquidity	Liquid	Lose liquidity when base rate goes down
Put option	None	After 1 year
Purchase limit	None	Capped
Buy in IRA	Yes	No
Tax deferred	No	Yes
Tax Free for Education	No	Yes, subject to income qualification

In general, serious investors prefer TIPS while small savers prefer I Bonds. I Bonds' annual purchase limit makes it difficult for someone with a large bond portfolio to switch into I Bonds. For serious investors, the higher yield on TIPS year after year makes up for the price fluctuation.

Interest Rate Changes

What happens to TIPS when interest rates change? It depends on what's driving the interest rate changes.

The nominal interest rate on a Treasury bond consists of two parts:

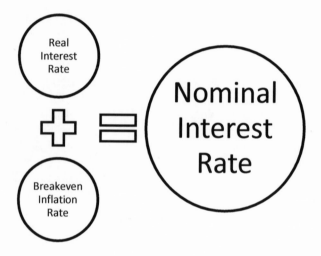

Real interest rate is what investors demand to earn after inflation.

Breakeven inflation rate is the difference between nominal interest rate and the real interest rate. If the nominal interest rate is 3% and the real interest rate is 1%, the breakeven inflation rate is 3% - 1% = 2%.

The breakeven inflation rate can be further divided into three components, although the exact value for each component is not observable separately.

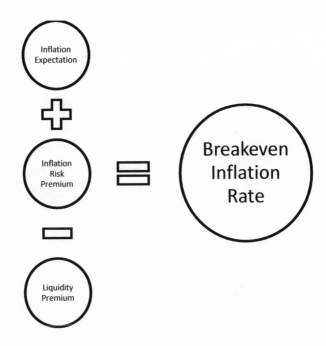

Inflation expectation is what investors expect the inflation to be during the life of the bond.

Inflation risk premium is the compensation for taking a risk on what the actual inflation will be versus the inflation expectation.

Liquidity premium is what investors give up for better liquidity in nominal Treasury bonds.

The nominal value of a TIPS bond is driven by two factors:

1. real interest rate
2. actual inflation rate

To see how the value of a TIPS bond will change in response to interest rate changes, we have to see which part of the interest rate changes. Of course more than one component can change at the same time and their effects could add to or offset one another.

I summarize the direction of changes in Table 3 on the next page. For the change in each component, I'm assuming the other components don't change ("all else being equal"). The last component, actual inflation rate, is not part of the nominal interest rate. I include it in the table because it affects the nominal value of a TIPS bond.

Table 3 Effect of Changes in Interest Rate Components

	Nominal Bonds		TIPS	
	Nominal Value	Real Value	Nominal Value	Real Value
real interest rate ↑	↓	↓	↓	↓
real interest rate ↓	↑	↑	↑	↑
inflation expectation ↑	↓	↓	no change	no change
inflation expectation ↓	↑	↑	no change	no change
inflation risk premium ↑	↓	↓	no change	no change
inflation risk premium ↓	↑	↑	no change	no change
liquidity premium ↑	↑	↑	no change	no change
liquidity premium ↓	↓	↓	no change	no change
actual inflation ↑	no change	↓	↑	no change
actual inflation ↓	no change	↑	↓	no change

Please note these are only the immediate effects. When you reinvest bond interest payments after interest rates go up, you will be able to earn more interest on the reinvestment. If you hold the bond long enough, you are better off with a higher interest rate than a lower one.

TIPS and Taxes

TIPS are bonds. Like interest from other bonds, interest paid from TIPS is taxed as ordinary income. The inflation adjustment to TIPS principal is also taxed as interest.

Because TIPS are Treasury bonds, the interest income is taxed as ordinary income for federal income tax but is exempt from state and local income taxes.

Although taxes on TIPS can be complicated, there are easy ways out.

The easiest way to handle taxes on TIPS is by putting them in a tax deferred or a tax free (Roth) account. Then you don't have to worry about taxes. There is no tax while they stay in a tax deferred or a tax free account. When you withdraw, you pay ordinary income tax on the withdrawal. It doesn't matter whether the withdrawal comes from TIPS, regular bonds, or stocks.

If you'd like to buy TIPS in a taxable account, another easy way to handle taxes is by buying them through a mutual fund or ETF (see Chapter 3). The mutual fund or

ETF will distribute taxable income to you. You pay taxes as you normally do for any other mutual fund or ETF.

Taxes get much more complicated if you buy individual TIPS in a taxable account. You must calculate income for each and every individual bond separately.

The interest paid to you during the year is taxed as ordinary income. The inflation adjustment to TIPS principal is also taxed as ordinary income, although it's not paid until the bond matures. It's treated as an Original Issue Discount (OID).

If there is deflation, not inflation, in one year, you get to deduct against the interest income you declared in the current year and previous years. If there is left-over negative OID, you carry it forward to future years.

The difference between the price you paid and the bond's face value must also be tracked. You may want to write it down over the life of the bond. The process is called *bond premium amortization*.

OID and bond premium amortization are covered in more detail in Chapter 6.

Risks in Investing in TIPS

TIPS are bonds. They have similar risks as other bonds. The most important risk in investing in TIPS is the interest rate risk.

Interest rate goes up. When nominal interest rate goes up, nominal bond prices go down. The nominal interest rate goes up for two reasons:

1. the breakeven inflation rate goes up
2. the real interest rate goes up

TIPS are not affected by the rise in the breakeven inflation rate because the principal and interest of TIPS are indexed to inflation. TIPS are affected by the changes in the real interest rate. If real interest rate goes up after you bought TIPS, the value of your TIPS bonds goes down.

Low inflation or deflation. If inflation turns out to be lower than expected, the return from TIPS will be lower than that from nominal bonds.

Some people call this a risk; I disagree. Buying TIPS is like buying insurance. You insure against the risk of unexpected inflation. If you had homeowner's insurance for many years and you never had a claim, you don't say your house not burnt down is a risk or buying insurance was a waste of money. You had insurance protection for all those years. That's the value of the insurance. It's the same with TIPS. Not having unexpected inflation is not a risk.

Your personal inflation rate may be higher than CPI changes. TIPS are indexed to the Consumer

Price Index (CPI). Inflation for your own consumption will be different. You may buy more food, energy, health care or higher education than their weight in the CPI. As a result you may experience a higher rate of inflation than the CPI changes.

TIPS will only protect you against CPI changes. There's no way to tie it to your personal inflation rate. But considering that other investments like nominal bonds don't even guarantee a rate of return above CPI changes, having some protection is still better than having no protection at all.

U.S. Dollar devaluation. TIPS are denominated in U.S. Dollars. If the U.S. Dollar devaluates against foreign currencies, your TIPS will buy fewer units of foreign goods or services.

To the extent the price changes are included in the CPI, you are protected. If they are not, you have this risk. This risk is not limited to TIPS. It also affects nominal bonds denominated in U.S. Dollars.

Taxes reduce inflation protection. You have to pay taxes on inflation. After taxes are paid, TIPS may not earn a rate of return above inflation. The higher the inflation rate, the lower the after-tax, after-inflation return from TIPS.

Nominal Treasury bonds are also affected by taxes. They may not have a positive after-tax, after-inflation return either. The higher the inflation rate, the lower their after-tax, after-inflation return.

How to Buy TIPS

You can buy TIPS in several different ways.

Mutual Funds. Just as there are mutual funds for stocks and other bonds, there are also mutual funds for TIPS. A TIPS mutual fund buys many TIPS bonds. You buy shares in the mutual fund. You own TIPS indirectly through the mutual fund.

The mutual fund manager decides which bonds to buy and when to buy and sell. As in other mutual funds, the mutual fund management company charges a percentage of the fund's assets for its service. The mutual fund company sets the initial minimum investment, usually a few thousand dollars. TIPS mutual funds are covered in more detail in Chapter 3.

ETFs. There are also Exchange Traded Funds (ETFs) for TIPS. ETFs work similarly to mutual funds, except you need a brokerage account to buy and sell ETFs.

ETFs trade all day whereas mutual funds price their shares once a day after the market closes. You will have to pay commissions for buying and selling ETFs unless your brokerage account gives you free trades. TIPS ETFs are also covered in more detail in Chapter 3.

Buy Individual TIPS at Auction. The Treasury Department sells TIPS to the public several times a year in auctions.

If you invest in a taxable account, you can buy TIPS directly from the U.S. Treasury through its TreasuryDirect program (*www.treasurydirect.gov*). If you invest in an IRA, you have to use a brokerage account. TIPS auctions are covered in more detail in Chapter 4.

Buy Individual TIPS On the Secondary Market. After TIPS are sold at auction, investors trade them with each other. This is called the secondary market.

Prices on the secondary market change all the time. You need a brokerage account to buy TIPS on the secondary market. You pay the prevailing price plus your brokerage firm's markup and commission. The secondary market is covered in more detail in Chapter 5.

Table 4 on the next page summarizes the various ways you can buy TIPS.

Table 4 Various Ways to Buy TIPS

	Mutual Fund Company	Brokerage Account	TreasuryDirect
IRA			
Mutual Fund	X	X	
ETF		X	
Individual TIPS - Auction		X	
Individual TIPS - Secondary Market		X	
Taxable Account			
Mutual Fund	X	X	
ETF		X	
Individual TIPS - Auction		X	X
Individual TIPS - Secondary Market		X	

Chapter 3 TIPS Funds and ETFs

In this chapter, you will explore:
- Investing in TIPS through a mutual fund or ETF versus purchasing individual bonds
- What the different yield numbers mean
- How a TIPS mutual fund or ETF makes distributions
- Choosing a TIPS mutual fund or ETF

Fund vs. Individual Bonds

A TIPS mutual fund or ETF is a great way to invest in TIPS. It offers convenience and diversification at a low cost. Buying TIPS through a mutual fund is a great idea. The advantages of buying TIPS through a mutual fund include:

Buy at any time without a transaction fee. You can buy shares in a TIPS mutual fund at any time without a transaction fee. Although there are ways to buy individual TIPS at auctions without a fee (see Chapter 4), the opportunities only come up a few times a year.

If you want to buy individual TIPS bonds when there's no auction, you must use a brokerage account and buy on the secondary market. Some brokerage firms charge a hefty commission for bond orders. For example the brokerage arm of mutual fund company Vanguard charges minimum $40 per order unless you have at least $1 million with Vanguard. You also pay a higher price ("markup") than the wholesale price when you buy on the secondary market. Or you will just have to wait until the next auction, but the price will have changed by then.

Instant diversification. A TIPS mutual fund holds many bonds with different maturities. You get all of them with a single purchase. If you are buying individual TIPS bonds, they don't come on auction at the same time. You must wait for the auctions or pay commissions and markups to establish your positions.

Sell at any time without a transaction fee. If you sell shares in a TIPS mutual fund, you normally receive the full value for each share, without having to pay a transaction fee. If you have individual TIPS bonds, there is no fee only if you wait until they mature. If you want to sell before they mature, you will have to incur a cost.

TreasuryDirect (page 35) charges $45; Vanguard charges at least $40. You also receive a lower price ("markdown") than the wholesale price when you sell on the secondary market.

Buy or sell for any random amount. Minimum additional investment in the *Vanguard Inflation-*

Protected Securities Fund (ticker: VIPSX) is $100. Want to buy $456.78? No problem. The individual TIPS bonds are in $100 increments at TreasuryDirect or in $1,000 increments in a brokerage account.

Reinvest interest payments immediately without charge. TIPS mutual funds typically offer automatic dividend reinvestment for free. If you have individual TIPS bonds, you must put the interest payments elsewhere. Reinvesting in another TIPS bond is also subject to the auction cycles and $100 increments at TreasuryDirect or $1,000 increments in a brokerage account.

The most convenient way to reinvest the interest payments from an individual TIPS is putting them into a TIPS mutual fund.

Easy tax handling for taxable accounts. Individual TIPS in a taxable account have a unique *phantom income* issue. Both the interest payments and the inflation adjustment are taxable, although the latter is not paid out until the bond matures. For more details, see *Original Issue Discount* on page 106 in Chapter 6.

A TIPS mutual fund shields that issue from the investor. You receive regular dividends from the fund and you get a 1099 form at the end of the year, just like you do when you invest in any other mutual fund.

All these conveniences come at a cost of 0.20% a year for the *Vanguard Inflation-Protected Securities*

Fund (ticker: VIPSX). That's $20 a year for each $10,000 invested. If you invest $100,000 or more in TIPS, Vanguard's fund offers Admiral shares (ticker VAIPX) at an expense ratio of 0.11%, or $11 a year per $10,000 invested.

The cost for investing in a TIPS mutual fund is very reasonable. Why bother buying individual bonds then? Because with individual bonds, you get:

Low expenses. If you buy at auctions and hold to maturity, there is no extra expense every year. If you buy a large amount of TIPS, you can save money by building your own TIPS ladder with individual bonds.

TreasuryDirect, Fidelity, Schwab, and E*Trade charge no fee or commission if you buy TIPS at auctions and hold to maturity. Even if you buy on the secondary market, when you buy long-term bonds in large quantities and you hold the bonds to maturity, a one-time commission and markup spread over many years can be less expensive than having to pay an ongoing expense year after year.

Be your own fund manager. You get to decide which TIPS bonds you buy.

When you buy fund shares you buy a basket. The fund's (experienced) managers decide what to buy and when to buy. With individual bonds, you become the (amateur) manager for your own fund. Want short maturities? Buy 5-year notes. Want long ones? Buy 30-year bonds.

Buying at auctions and holding to maturity is not that hard. I will give you a step-by-step guide in Chapter 4. But you still can't beat the liquidity and convenience from a mutual fund. Buying TIPS through a mutual fund is more convenient and very cost-effective.

Understand Yield Numbers

When you buy a TIPS mutual fund or ETF, you may ask *"What's the yield?"* If you look up the information on Morningstar or on the provider's website, you will see several different yield numbers. What's going on?

Let's use as an example the most popular TIPS mutual fund, *Vanguard Inflation-Protected Securities Fund* (ticker: VIPSX). On February 20, 2010, Morningstar reported its yield was 1.68%. Vanguard's website showed the yield as 0.74%.

The 1.68% yield number from Morningstar is more than double the 0.74% yield number from Vanguard. Who was right?

Here's how Morningstar explains how it reports the yield:

> "Morningstar computes yield by dividing the sum of the fund's income distributions (interest distributions from fixed-income securities, divi-

dends from stocks, and realized gains from currency transactions) for the past 12 months by the previous month's NAV (adjusted upward for any capital gains distributed over the same time period)."

Vanguard explains its number with these two pop-up notes:

"E -- BASED ON HOLDINGS' YIELD TO MATURITY FOR 30 DAYS AS OF END OF PREVIOUS WEEK.

"G -- DOES NOT INCLUDE ANY INCOME ADJUSTMENT RESULTING FROM CHANGE IN INFLATION RATE"

Got it? Morningstar reports distribution yield over the trailing 12 months. Vanguard reports yield to maturity over the trailing 30 days. Vanguard's number is also a real yield, without inflation adjustment, while Morningstar's number includes inflation adjustment.

The 12-month trailing distribution yield from Morningstar looks backwards. It calculates from what the fund paid out in the last 12 months. Due to market changes, what the fund will pay in the next 12 months will not be the same as what it did in the previous 12 months. The payout is not a good metric for a TIPS fund anyway, because it includes inflation adjustments. Based on the number alone, you can't know how the fund paid or will pay relative to inflation.

The yield to maturity number from Vanguard is more meaningful. It looks forward to all the expected interest and principal repayments from the bonds in the fund. It then calculates a necessary rate of return that would generate the same cash flows at the current prices. Because it's forward-looking and it's net of inflation adjustment, an investor can use this number as a measure for how much inflation protection the fund is providing.

There is a small problem with the yield to maturity number from Vanguard. It's an average over the past 30 days as of the end of the previous week. If the yield has been stable, it's not much of a problem. If the yield has risen or fallen sharply recently, the average will be lower or higher than what the yield is today.

When you buy a fund, you are getting today's yield, not its yield over the last 30 days. The 30-day average number can make the fund look better or worse than the yield on an individual bond of similar maturity, when in fact they are comparable.

ETF provider iShares provides more granularities in the yield data for its ETF *iShares Barclays TIPS Bond Fund* (ticker: TIP). It reports the distribution yield, the 30-day SEC yield, and the real yield. This last number is the real yield to maturity on the as-of date, and it's the most meaningful yield number for someone who is considering buying the ETF.

Distributions

In a taxable account, investing in a TIPS mutual fund or ETF has two advantages over investing in a basket of individual TIPS bonds: cash flow and the ease of tax reporting.

A TIPS fund pays out both the interest earned and the inflation adjustment. The fund's shareholders report these distributions as taxable interest in the same way as they do for any other bond fund.

These distributions are called "dividend" but they have nothing to do with stock dividend. They are taxed as ordinary income for federal income tax. Because the interest income originates from the U.S. Treasury, it's exempt from state and local income taxes.

If an investor owns individual bonds, the inflation adjustments in those TIPS bonds are not paid out until the bonds mature. In a TIPS mutual fund or ETF, because the inflation adjustments are taxable, the fund must pay them out to the shareholders.

If the Treasury does not pay out the inflation adjustments to the TIPS fund, where does the fund get the money to pay the inflation adjustments to the fund's shareholders?

The money can come from several sources. First, not all the distributions are really paid out. Many investors automatically reinvest distributions. For the fund, the reinvested distributions go out and come back on paper; no actual cash leaves the fund. The interest payments the fund received from the bonds may very well be sufficient to pay the shareholders who don't automatically reinvest distributions.

Second, there are incoming purchases from investors. Instead of using 100% of the new money to buy more bonds, the fund can save a small percentage aside for the expected distributions.

Then there are matured bonds. The fund doesn't have to invest 100% of the proceeds into new bonds. If it needs money for distributions, it can reserve some money for that purpose and reinvest the rest.

Finally, there are sales proceeds. During the normal operation of the fund, the fund buys and sells bonds. If the fund estimates that it needs money for distributions, it can sell some bonds or just set aside some money from the sales proceeds.

How the fund comes up with the money for distributions isn't very important to the fund investors. A TIPS fund or ETF investor only needs to know that in a taxable account, there will be distributions for all taxable income and that the fund or ETF makes it easier to report and pay taxes.

Open-End TIPS Mutual Funds

An investor can buy shares in an open-end TIPS mutual fund directly from the fund company without a brokerage account. With a brokerage account, an investor can buy funds from different mutual fund companies.

A search on Morningstar returned more than 60 funds in the "Inflation-Protected Bond" category with no load, a minimum initial investment of $10,000 or less, and an expense ratio of 1.0% or less. That's plenty to choose from.

Table 5 on the next page shows some of the most popular funds (by total assets), as well as some funds from the largest retail mutual fund families. When a fund has multiple share classes, I'm showing the expense ratio for the share class with the lowest initial investment requirement.

Table 5 Select Open-End TIPS Mutual Funds

Fund	Expense Ratio	Total Assets ($ million)
Vanguard Inflation-Protected Securities Fund (VIPSX)	0.20%	28,863
PIMCO Real Return Fund D (PRRDX)	0.88%	17,451
American Century Inflation-Adjusted Bond Fund (ACITX)	0.49%	3,261
Fidelity Inflation-Protected Bond Fund (FINPX)	0.45%	2,721
BlackRock Inflation Protected Bond Fund (BPRSX)	0.66%	2,562
Hartford Inflation Plus Fund (HIPIX)	0.60%	1,754
TIAA-CREF Inflation Link Bond Fund Retail (TCILX)	0.49%	884
T. Rowe Price Inflation Protected Bond Fund (PRIPX)	0.50%	316
Schwab Inflation Protected Fund (SWRSX)	0.50%	304

* Retrieved using Morningstar Fund Screener on Feb. 15, 2010.

More dollars are invested in the *Vanguard Inflation-Protected Securities Fund* (ticker: VIPSX) than any other fund in this group. It's ten times the size of the Fidelity fund and almost 100 times the size of the T. Rowe Price fund. There's a very good reason for that: the Vanguard fund has the lowest expense ratio.

The Vanguard fund basically invests in all the TIPS bonds in the market. As of December 31, 2009, there were 28 TIPS outstanding from the U.S. Treasury with a maturity over one year. The Vanguard fund owned 26.

To me, the Vanguard fund looks like a reasonable choice with low expenses: nothing fancy, just a plain vanilla TIPS fund. If you'd like to get more information about this fund, visit *vanguard.com* or call Vanguard at 1-877-662-7447.

TIPS ETFs

There are far fewer TIPS ETFs than there are open-end TIPS mutual funds. As of February 2010, there were only five TIPS ETFs in the market.

Table 6 TIPS ETFs

ETF	Expense Ratio	Trading Volume	Total Assets ($ million)
iShares Barclays TIPS Bond ETF (TIP)	0.20%	1,166,490	19,460
SPDR Barclays Capital TIPS ETF (IPE)	0.18%	54,501	353
PIMCO Broad U.S. TIPS Index Fund (TIPZ)	0.20%	3,965	22
PIMCO 1-5 Year U.S. TIPS Index Fund (STPZ)	0.20%	61,826	207
PIMCO 15+ Year U.S. TIPS Index Fund (LTPZ)	0.20%	4,618	21

* Retrieved from iShares and SPDR web sites on Feb. 20, 2010. Trading volume data were the average daily trading volume in the previous three months from Yahoo! Finance.

In terms of total assets and trading volume, *iShares Barclays TIPS Bond ETF* (ticker: TIP) absolutely dominates the other TIPS ETFs. A higher trading volume leads to higher liquidity and a smaller trading cost. The *SPDR Barclays Capital TIPS ETF* (ticker: IPE) and *PIMCO Broad US TIPS ETF* (ticker: TIPZ) have similar objectives and portfolio holdings as the iShares ETF TIP, except for their much smaller assets and trading volume.

Similar to the open-end fund *Vanguard Inflation-Protected Securities Fund* (ticker: VIPSX), the iShares ETF invests in substantially all TIPS in the market. As of December 31, 2009, it held all 28 outstanding TIPS with a maturity longer than one year. Its portfolio holdings were very similar to that of the Vanguard fund.

Table 7 Portfolio Comparison: TIP vs. VIPSX

Maturity	iShares TIPS ETF (TIP)	Vanguard TIPS Fund (VIPSX)
< 5 years	36%	38%
5 - 10 years	34%	34%
> 10 years	29%	27%

* Compiled from portfolio holdings data as of Dec. 31, 2009 obtained from iShares and Vanguard websites.

The iShares TIPS ETF can be a good alternative to the Vanguard open-end TIPS mutual fund if an investor prefers to use an ETF or if someone can invest in an ETF more cost efficiently than in an open-end mutual fund. Most discount brokerage firms charge a lower commission for ETF trades that they do for mutual fund orders. Fidelity Investments customers can trade TIP for free.

The typical disadvantages for investing in an ETF also apply to investing in a TIPS ETF. Brokerage commissions on small trades can make it more expensive than investing in an open-end mutual fund. The bid-ask spread and the possible premium to Net Asset Value can impose additional costs to investing in TIPS through an ETF.

Bond manager PIMCO came out with three new TIPS ETFs in September 2009. Although PIMCO usually actively manages its bond portfolios with regard to quality, maturity, and individual issue selections, these ETFs are managed to track an index. All three PIMCO TIPS ETFs have an expense ratio of 0.20% per year.

PIMCO 1-5 Year U.S. TIPS Index Fund (ticker: STPZ) invests in TIPS maturing in one to five years. Of the 30 TIPS bonds outstanding as of December 31, 2009, 10 bonds would mature between one year and five years. STPZ held all 10.

PIMCO 15+ Year U.S. TIPS Index Fund (ticker: LTPZ) invests in TIPS maturing in 15 years or more. Of the 30 TIPS bonds outstanding as of December 31, 2009, eight bonds would mature in 15 years or more. LTPZ held all eight.

PIMCO Broad U.S. TIPS Index Fund (TIPZ) invests in TIPS maturing in one year or more. Of the 30 TIPS bonds outstanding as of December 31, 2009, 28 bonds had a maturity date greater than one year. TIPZ held all 28.

PIMCO's TIPZ is similar to iShares' TIP in both holdings and expense ratio. Because TIPZ is new to the marketplace while TIP has been established for some time, iShares' TIP still holds an advantage in trading volume and bid-ask spread.

PIMCO's short and long TIPS ETFs STPZ and LTPZ are unique in the market. There are no open-end mutual funds or other ETFs that invest in only short-term or long-term TIPS. If an investor wishes to target either short or long end of the maturity range, STPZ and LTPZ are a good substitute for purchasing individual TIPS on the secondary market.

Chapter 4 Individual TIPS - Auctions

TIPS mutual funds or ETFs are a convenient and cost-effective way to invest in TIPS. Some investors will appreciate the ultimate control and the lower long-term cost of ownership of investing in individual TIPS.

Investing in individual TIPS is more complicated than investing in a TIPS mutual fund or ETF. The investor basically works as the manager of his or her fund.

I will explain the details of investing in individual TIPS in the next two chapters. First let me introduce a few more terms for individual bonds.

Bond Lingo

A Treasury bond with maturity up to 1 year is officially called a Treasury *Bill*.

A Treasury bond with a maturity greater than 1 year but no more than 10 years is officially called a Treasury *Note*.

A Treasury bond with a maturity greater than 10 years is officially called a Treasury *Bond*.

There are no TIPS Bills at this time, only TIPS Notes and TIPS Bonds. Why they make that distinction and give different names by maturity is beyond me. In this book I will just use the generic term *bond* (lower case b). When I say "bond" I mean both Notes and Bonds.

The stated interest rate on a bond is called the *coupon* rate. A TIPS bond pays interest twice a year based on the coupon rate.

The principal value of a bond is called *par*. If a bond sells for a price higher than par, it's said to be selling at a *premium*. If a bond sells for a price lower than par, it's said to be selling at a *discount*.

Yield to Maturity is the necessary internal rate of return that will discount the bond's cash flows to its selling price (see page 5). When people talk about the yield on a bond, they are usually referring to its yield to maturity. When a bond sells at a premium, the yield is lower than the coupon. When it sells at a discount, the yield is higher than the coupon.

In bond convention, *1 bond* means $1,000 in face value. When you buy individual TIPS in a brokerage account, your typical minimum and incremental investment is 1 bond. Some brokers require minimum 5 bonds or 10 bonds.

How TIPS Are Issued

TIPS are issued by the U.S. Treasury. In the second month of every quarter: February, May, August, and November, the Office of Debt Management in the

Treasury Department holds a meeting on how the government will borrow and fund its operations.

The meeting is called the quarterly refunding meeting. After the meeting, they will publish a calendar that lists the dates and the types of debt the government will sell in the next few months.

The actual selling is done by a single-price Dutch auction. A few days before the actual auction date, the Treasury Department makes an announcement about what and how much it will sell. The auction will close at a set time.

The bond dealers will submit bids for what yield they will accept and the quantity they want. These bids are called *competitive bids*. Others, including the general public, also can submit orders but they can't specify a desired yield. These orders are called *noncompetitive bids*. The noncompetitive bidders will accept whatever the final price comes out to be.

Here's a hypothetical example. Suppose the Treasury Department is selling $9 billion TIPS and it receives six competitive bids plus a number of noncompetitive bids as follows:

Table 8 Hypothetical Treasury Auction Bids

Bidder	Yield	Quantity
A	2.1%	$2 billion
B	2.2%	$3 billion
C	2.3%	$2 billion
D	2.4%	$3 billion
E	2.5%	$2 billion
F	2.6%	$2 billion
noncompetitive bids	N/A	$0.5 billion

The final yield from this auction will be 2.4%. That's the lowest yield at which Treasury will be able to sell all $9 billion (the auction "clears").

Every successful bidder will receive the same yield but not all bidders will receive the full quantity they wanted. Bidders A, B, and C will get the full quantity they bid, because their bids are higher than the final price (lower yield). Noncompetitive bidders will get their $0.5 billion. Bidder D will get only $1.5 billion even though it wants $3 billion. Bidders E and F will get nothing because their bids are too low.

$$2 + 3 + 2 + 1.5 + 0.5 = 9$$

In a Treasury auction, retail investors take a free ride with noncompetitive bids. They will always receive the same yield as successful competitive bidders. They will always get all the bonds they want. Noncompetitive bids are a very good deal.

Why Auctions?

There are several good reasons to buy TIPS directly from the U.S. Treasury at one of its auctions.

Although your noncompetitive bid in a TIPS auction sounds like complete lack of control — you take whatever price it comes out to be — it's actually one of the best features of a Treasury auction.

All orders — from the big financial institutions buying millions of dollars, and from you for a few thousand dollars — get the same price from the auction. Your small order for $1,000 is treated the same as a $100 million order from a bank. Actually your order is treated a little better because you are guaranteed to receive the full quantity of your order while some big guys who bid too low either won't get any bond at all or will get a smaller quantity than they wanted.

Being able to buy TIPS at wholesale prices is the primary reason for buying TIPS at auction.

Another good reason for buying TIPS at auction is that the bonds sold at auction are either brand new or issued within the last few months. Because they are "fresh" they don't have a lot of accumulated inflation in their principal. They have better protection for deflation. See *TIPS and Deflation* on page 100 for more details on how deflation affects TIPS.

A disadvantage of buying TIPS at auction is that you have to wait for the scheduled auctions. Auctions don't come very often. If you missed the date, you will have to wait for the next one. The choice of maturity is limited to what Treasury chooses to sell. You also won't know the exact price or yield before you decide to buy. If you are willing to live with these limitations, buying TIPS at auction is a great way to invest in individual TIPS.

Which Account

If you are going to buy TIPS at auction in a *taxable* account, you can set up a free online account directly with the U.S. Treasury through its TreasuryDirect service.

You link a bank account to TreasuryDirect. All your purchases will be debited from your linked bank account. There is no fee for buying TIPS through TreasuryDirect. The minimum purchase amount is low: just $100. Visit TreasuryDirect on the Internet at *treasurydirect.gov* where you can view a guided tour and open an account.

However, if you wish to buy TIPS in an IRA, you can't do it with TreasuryDirect because the Treasury Department is not in the business of acting as an IRA custodian. A TreasuryDirect account has to be a taxable account.

If you'd like to buy TIPS at auction in an IRA, you will have to use a brokerage account. Fidelity, Schwab, and E*Trade are good choices because they don't charge any fee for buying TIPS at auction as long as the order is placed online. You can also buy from Vanguard Brokerage Service, but you may have to pay a fee unless you have over $100,000 with Vanguard.

Table 9 on the next page shows the fees and minimum purchase amount for buying TIPS at auction through TreasuryDirect and several discount brokerage firms. The minimum increment investment at most brokerage firms is 1 bond or $1,000 in face value. At TreasuryDirect, it's $100.

Table 9 Fees and Minimum Purchase Amount at TreasuryDirect and Some Brokerage Firms

	Minimum Purchase	Fee - Online	Fee - By Phone
TreasuryDirect	$100	Free	N/A[1]
Fidelity	$1,000	Free	$20
Schwab	$1,000	Free	$25
E*Trade	$1,000	Free	$20
Vanguard	$10,000	$10[2]	$25[3]
TD Ameritrade	$5,000	$25	$25
WellsTrade	$1,000	N/A[4]	$49

* Compiled in December 2009 from information on providers' web sites and conversions with customer service representatives.

Notes:

1. TreasuryDirect is a 100% online system. There's also a Legacy Treasury Direct service which takes phone orders but certain maturities are not available through Legacy Treasury Direct. Call 800-722-2678.

2. Free for customers with at least $100,000 in Vanguard funds and ETFs.

3. $15 for customers with at least $100,000 in Vanguard funds and ETFs. Free for clients with at least $1 million.

4. WellsTrade does not take online orders for TIPS auctions.

The rest of this chapter is a step-by-step guide for buying TIPS from Treasury auctions:

1. Know the Schedule
2. Read the Announcement
3. Place Order
4. Read the Results

Know the Schedule

After you decide which account to use, you will have to know when the Treasury Department will hold an auction and which maturity they will sell. Currently the Treasury Department sells TIPS by auctions only a few times a year. Table 10 on the next page shows the auction schedule as of February 2010.

Table 10 TIPS Auction Schedule as of February 2010

	5-Year	10-Year	30-Year*
January		1N	
February			2N
April	2N	1R	
July		1N	
October	2R	1R	

1 = auction date in the first half of the month
2 = auction date in the second half of the month
N = a new issue
R = a reopening

* In November 2009, Treasury announced they will disconti-
nue issuing 20-year TIPS and start issuing 30-year TIPS.
More changes to the auction schedule are forthcoming.

A *new issue* means the bond is brand new. It has
never been sold before.

A *reopening* means selling additional quantities of
an existing bond. The coupon rate will be the same but
the yield will be different.

For example, the schedule table shows that in the
month of April, there is an auction for a 10-year TIPS in
the first half of the month. It's a reopening of the same

TIPS first sold in January. It's really a 9-year 9-month TIPS to be exact. Then in the second half of the month, there is an auction for a new 5-year TIPS.

The Treasury Department publishes a tentative auction schedule with exact dates a few months in advance. Although it is said to be tentative, the schedule is pretty much set once it's published. The schedule is available online at:

http://www.ustreas.gov/offices/domestic-finance/
debt-management/auctions/

The published schedule includes auctions for both nominal Treasury bonds and TIPS. The TIPS auctions are shaded in a different color so they are easy to spot.

There are three dates in the published schedule.

Announcement Date. This is when the Treasury Department makes an official announcement with more details about the bond being auctioned. You can't place an order until the Announcement Date.

Auction Date. The Auction Date is the date when the auction actually happens.

Settlement Date. The Settlement Date is the date when you pay and receive the bonds. You must have enough cash ready on this date.

Read the Announcement

A few days before the auction actually happens, the Treasury Department publishes an official auction announcement on their website. The URL for this website is:

> http://treasurydirect.gov/instit/annceresult/press/
> press_secannpr.htm

The announcement lists the key terms for the bond that will be auctioned. You should read the announcement before you decide to buy from the auction.

Estimate the Yield. You will not know what the yield will be until the auction is over, but you can take a guess using the current yield on existing bonds that are traded on the secondary market.

I use the *Daily Treasury Real Yield Curve Rates* published by the Treasury Department. The data are available online at:

> http://www.treas.gov/offices/domestic-finance/
> debt-management/interest-rate/real_yield.shtml

I also use the *Treasury Inflation-Indexed Security, Constant Maturity* yield charts from the Federal Reserve Bank of St. Louis. There are charts for 5-year, 7-year, 10-year, and 20-year TIPS. After Treasury starts selling 30-year TIPS in 2010, there will probably be charts for 30-year TIPS as well. The URLs for these charts are listed in the Appendix on page 121.

Figure 6: 10-Year TIPS Yields 2003-2009
Source: Federal Reserve Bank of St. Louis

The yield from the auction should be close to the yields on similar bonds on the market, give or take daily market fluctuations. Remember the number is the real yield, which is above and beyond inflation.

You have to decide yourself whether it's a good yield for you or not. Typically if the yield is above 3%, it's considered a great yield. If it's below 1%, it's not so good.

If you are interested in buying from the upcoming auction and you'd like to get a handle on how much money you will need for each bond, you will need some data from the official announcement to do the calculation.

New Issue versus Reopening. Sometimes the auction is a new issue. Sometimes it's a reopening.

A new issue means the bond is brand new. It has never been sold before.

The coupon rate on a new issue bond will be determined at auction. The coupon rate will be set to the nearest 0.125% at or below the high yield in the auction. If the high yield is zero or negative, the coupon rate will be set to zero. The purchase price will be adjusted accordingly. For example if the yield from the auction is 1.485%, the coupon will be rounded down to 1.375%.

A reopening means the Treasury Department will sell additional quantities of an existing bond they sold before.

The coupon rate on a reopened bond is already known. It was set in the previous auction. The auction for the reopening will determine only the yield and price.

The auction announcement will indicate if the auction is for a new issue or for a reopening.

Another difference between a new issue and a reopening is the inflation adjustment. Because a reopened bond has been on the market for some time, it has accumulated some inflation adjustment. A reopened bond typically costs slightly more in nominal dollars than a new issue unless its coupon rate is significantly below the current market yield.

Important Dates and Index Ratio. The official auction announcement contains many data points but only these are relevant for estimating how much a bond will cost.

- **Issue Date**: the date you will officially own the bond
- **Maturity Date**: the date the U.S. Treasury will pay you back
- **Dated Date**: the date from which interest will be calculated
- **Interest Rate** (reopening only, not applicable to new issues): the coupon rate
- **Index Ratio**: the CPI value on the Issue Date divided by the CPI value on the Dated Date

Estimate Dollars Needed. I made a spreadsheet that estimates the total dollars needed, taking into consideration the index ratio and accrued interest. If you plug in the data you gathered from above, together with your yield estimate into my spreadsheet, you will see roughly how much you will need for each bond. The spreadsheet is available online at

http://thefinancebuff.com/go/tips-auction-spreadsheet

Place Order

Say you decided to buy some TIPS at auction. How do you place your order? It depends on which account you use.

If you are going to buy TIPS in a taxable account, you can buy them from TreasuryDirect. If you want to buy in an IRA, you have to use a brokerage account. You can't set up an IRA with TreasuryDirect.

TreasuryDirect has a guided tour on its website *www.treasurydirect.gov* that shows you how to create an account and place an order. TreasuryDirect requires a minimum purchase of $100 in face value.

In Vanguard Brokerage Service, click on the link for *View and trade bonds or CDs*, then *Treasury Auction*. Vanguard Brokerage Service requires a minimum order of 10 bonds or $10,000 in face value. If you have questions about how to place an order, call the bond desk at 800-669-0514.

In Fidelity, it's under *Trade Fixed Income*, then *Search Inventory*, then *TIPS (Auction)*. The minimum order size at Fidelity is 1 bond or $1,000 in face value. If you have questions, call their fixed income specialists at 800-544-5372.

Enter the number of bonds you'd like to buy (1 bond = $1,000 in face value). You can't specify any price limit because your order will be a non-competitive bid.

The exact cutoff time for the auction will be specified in the official announcement. It's usually around 12:00 p.m. Eastern Time. Your order must be received before the auction cutoff time on the auction date.

If you place your order in a brokerage account, the brokerage firm imposes its own cutoff time before the official cutoff time to allow itself sufficient time to transmit your order to the Treasury.

For example the cutoff time at Vanguard Brokerage Service is usually 9:30 a.m. Eastern Time for online orders or 10:00 a.m. Eastern Time for phone orders. To play it safe, it's better to place the order by the close of business day before the auction date.

Read the Auction Result

A few hours after the auction closes, the Treasury Department publishes an auction result announcement on their web site. They also keep an archive of the results from previous auctions. The URL is:

http://treasurydirect.gov/instit/annceresult/press/
press_secannpr.htm

There are many numbers in the auction result. You should pay particular attention to four numbers and one date.

High Yield. This is the most important number from the auction. It's the yield you will earn from investing in this bond. It also determines the price you pay for the bond.

Interest Rate. For a new issue, the Interest Rate is the High Yield rounded *down* to the nearest 0.125%. If the High Yield is 0% or less, the Interest Rate will stay at 0%. This number determines how much interest the bond will pay every six months.

For a reopening, the Interest Rate was determined when the bond was sold in the previous auction. It was already known before the auction for the reopening started.

The High Yield from the auction for a reopening may be higher or lower than the Interest Rate. When the High Yield is higher than the Interest Rate, the bond is sold at a discount (price less than the face value). When the High Yield is lower than the Interest Rate, the bond is sold at a premium (price greater than the face value).

Adjusted Price and Adjusted Accrued Interest per \$1,000. These two numbers determine the amount of money you need to pay for each bond. It's calculated as follows:

Cash needed per bond =
    Adjusted Price * 10 + Adjusted Accrued Interest per \$1,000

Do the calculation and multiply it by the number of bonds you ordered. Make sure you have enough money in your account by the Issue Date.

Table 11 shows the auction result for a 10-year TIPS in April 2009:

Table 11 Auction result for 10-year TIPS, April 7, 2009

Interest Rate	2-1/8%
High Yield	1.589%
Adjusted Price	103.325496
Adjusted Accrued Interest per $1,000	$5.20771

First notice because the auction was for a reopening, there was a big difference between the High Yield and the Interest Rate. When this same bond was sold in January 2009, the High Yield was 2.245%. The Interest Rate was set at that time to 2.125% (2.245% rounded down to nearest 0.125%). The market conditions changed in three months. When the same bond was sold again in April, the yield dropped to 1.589%.

In this example the Adjusted Price was 103.325496; the Adjusted Accrued Interest per $1,000 was $5.20771. Therefore the amount of money needed for each $1,000 bond bought at this auction was:

Adjusted Price * 10 + Adjusted Accrued Interest per $1,000
= 103.325496 * 10 + 5.20771
= 1,038.46267

If you ordered 20 bonds, you will need

1,038.46267 * 20 = $20,769.25

Issue Date. This is the date when you will officially own the bond. It's also the date when you have to pay for your order. It's usually a few days after the auction date. Make sure you have enough cash in your account on this date.

That's it. If you follow these steps:

1. Know the Schedule
2. Read the Announcement
3. Place Order
4. Read the Results

you will become a proud owner of some TIPS you bought directly from a Treasury auction.

Chapter 5 Individual TIPS - Secondary Market

Buying TIPS directly through Treasury auctions is a great way to invest in individual TIPS. However, there are still some limitations. The secondary market can help you overcome these limitations. In this chapter, you will explore:

- What is the secondary market
- Why you should consider buying TIPS on the secondary market
- What the numbers in a quote mean
- How to decide when, which issue, and where you would buy
- Selling TIPS before they mature

What Is the Secondary Market?

Buying TIPS on the secondary market means you are buying the bonds from other people who already own them, very much like buying a "pre-owned" car.

Actually most of the stock market is secondary market. Except in Initial Public Offerings, when you buy a stock you are buying from another investor who already owns the stock.

After the U.S. Treasury sells the bonds at auction, the owners of these bonds can trade them with other investors. Bond dealers make a market in these bonds. They advertise a price at which they are willing to buy (the *bid price*) and a slightly higher price at which they are willing to sell (the *ask price*).

This is also very similar to how the stock market works. Like stocks, market prices for bonds also change every minute. But unlike stocks, there is no formal exchange for bonds. Bonds are said to trade "over the counter" although there is no physical counter to speak of. Because there is no formal exchange, retail investors usually can't get the current market price by the minute when they buy bonds.

Only brokers and institutions buying and selling millions of dollars worth of bonds can see the market prices on their Bloomberg terminals. Retail investors can only buy from brokers who often add a markup to the market price.

For many investors, it's not necessary to buy on the secondary market because it's much simpler to buy at auctions or through a mutual fund. However, for experienced investors, the secondary market provides some unique opportunities.

Why Buy on the Secondary Market?

When you buy TIPS at auction, you are buying directly from the issuer, the U.S. Treasury. You pay the same price as the institutions. There is no markup in auctions. Then why should any investor even consider buying on the secondary market? Because most of the time they have no better choice.

The Treasury Department only holds TIPS auctions a few times a year (see auction schedule on page 62). The secondary market is open all year round. Sometimes the prices are attractive but there is no auction. If you want to take advantage of the attractive prices, you have to buy on the secondary market.

When the Treasury Department holds an auction, they only sell one specific bond. The secondary market has all the issues trading all the time. If Treasury is doing an auction for a short-term bond but you want a long-term bond, you have two choices: (1) wait or (2) buy it on the secondary market.

When you buy on the secondary market, you are buying from an existing owner. You need a brokerage account. You can't do it in TreasuryDirect. An account with most name-brand brokerage firms will work. Some small online discount brokers can't handle bond orders. Different brokerage firms have different pricing and commission schedules.

Understand TIPS Quotes

The price and yield quotes are perhaps the source of most confusion about buying individual TIPS on the secondary market. Unlike nominal bonds, TIPS are quoted in real price and real yield while the actual purchase is done with nominal dollars.

Let's use an actual quote from a broker for one specific bond as an example. Table 12 on the next page shows a quote I received from Fidelity Investments in December 2009.

Table 12 Sample Quote for a TIPS bond on the Secondary Market

Description	UNITED STATES TREAS NTS 1.37500% 07/15/2018 TIPS
Coupon	1.375
Maturity Date	07/15/2018
Price	
Bid	100.710
Ask	100.992
Yield	
Bid	1.287
Ask	1.252
Inflation Factor	1.00193
Adjusted Price	
Bid	100.904370
Ask	101.186914

There are a lot of numbers. Let me explain what they mean.

Coupon: 1.375. It means this bond will pay interest at an annual rate of 1.375% of inflation adjusted principal. TIPS pay interest twice a year.

Maturity Date: 07/15/2018. This is when the inflation adjusted principal will be paid back to you.

You can also tell by the maturity date when the bond will pay interest. TIPS always pay the last interest on the maturity date. Therefore this bond will pay interest on January 15 and July 15 every year.

Price, Bid and Ask: 100.710/100.992. The bid price is the price the dealer pays you when you sell. The ask price is the price you pay the dealer when you buy. The bid price is always lower than the ask price. When you are buying, pay attention to the ask price (the higher of the two).

These numbers are expressed as a percentage of inflation adjusted principal (see *Inflation Factor* on the next page). The ask price of 100.992 means you will pay 100.992% of the inflation adjusted principal if you buy this bond from the dealer.

Some brokers display the prices in a number followed by a multiple of 1/32. For example 100-31 means the whole number 100 plus 31/32, which is 100.96875 in decimal.

Yield, Bid and Ask: 1.287/1.252. These are real Yield to Maturity (YTM) expressed in percentages.

YTM is an internal rate of return calculation for all the cash flows from a bond (see page 5). A real YTM is calculated using cash flows in real terms.

The bid yield is the yield you give up when you sell. The ask yield is the yield you receive when you buy. The ask yield is always lower than the bid yield. When you are buying, pay attention to the ask yield (the lower of the two).

For the bond in our example, if you buy at the broker's ask price of 100.992, your real YTM is 1.252%.

Inflation Factor: 1.00193. This is unique to TIPS. The principal value of a TIPS bond is adjusted by this multiplier. It's also called the *index ratio*. See *How TIPS Are Adjusted for Inflation* on page 100 for more information.

The inflation adjusted principal is $1,000 multiplied by the index ratio. Therefore the inflation adjusted principal for this bond in our example is $1,001.93. The ever changing index ratio makes your bond keep up with inflation and deflation.

Adjusted Price, Bid and Ask: 100.904370 / 101.186914. These are the bid and ask prices multiplied by the inflation factor also known as the index ratio.

If you multiply the ask price of 100.992 by the index ratio of 1.00193, you get 101.186914. Because they are a simple multiplication, not all brokers display these in their quotes. Fidelity is showing these numbers here for the investors' convenience.

There is one more piece of data that's not shown in the quote. It's called *accrued interest*. Accrued interest is the interest since the last interest payment date.

After you buy the bond, you will receive six months worth of interest on the next interest payment date. But because the current owner owned it between the last interest payment date and the day before you bought the bond, it's only fair that they receive a portion of the interest.

Therefore when you buy the bond from the current owner, you have to pay them the interest they already earned. Because it's simply an advance from the next interest payment, accrued interest is usually not included in the price quote.

So altogether, the broker's quote on page 77 is showing you that if you accept the quote and buy this bond, you will have a bond that

- matures on July. 15, 2018;
- pays 1.375% annual interest rate multiplied by the ever changing inflation adjusted principal;
- has an inflation adjusted principal of $1,001.93;
- costs 100.992% of the inflation adjusted principal ($1,001.93) plus accrued interest;
- gives you a real yield to maturity of 1.252% before broker commission

In addition to these numbers in the quote, if you use my online spreadsheet at

http://thefinancebuff.com/go/tips-secondary-market/

you will also see

- the all-in cost including accrued interest and brokerage commission;
- your real yield to maturity after you pay the brokerage commission

When to Buy

As with any other investment, you want to buy TIPS when prices are low and yields are high. There are several places on the Internet where you can monitor the TIPS market.

Wall Street Journal, *TIPS Market Data*:

http://online.wsj.com/mdc/public/page/2_3020-tips.html

This web page shows market yield on specific TIPS issues. It's updated once a day after the market closes. It also keeps an archive of the prices and yields in the past. The prices on this page use the 1/32 convention. 99.01 means 99 plus 1/32, which equals 99.03125 in decimal.

Bloomberg, *Government Bonds*:

http://www.bloomberg.com/markets/rates/

Instead of showing the yield on every TIPS issue, Bloomberg lists the yield for only four issues as a representative sample. It's updated in real time when the market is open.

U.S. Treasury, *Daily Treasury Real Yield Curve Rates*:

http://www.treas.gov/offices/domestic-finance/
    debt-management/interest-rate/real_yield.shtml

This web page from U.S. Treasury lists constant maturity yields for four maturities. The yields are extrapolated to exactly 5 years, 7 years, 10 years, and 20 years even if there are no bonds that actually mature at those exact marks. The data are updated daily after the market closes.

Federal Reserve Bank of St. Louis publishes TIPS yield charts. Using the same constant maturity yields data from the U.S. Treasury, these charts show where the yields have been in the recent past.

5-Year Treasury Inflation-Indexed Security, Constant Maturity:

http://research.stlouisfed.org/fred2/series/
    DFII5?cid=82

7-Year Treasury Inflation-Indexed Security, Constant Maturity:

http://research.stlouisfed.org/fred2/series/
    DFII7?cid=82

10-Year Treasury Inflation-Indexed Security, Constant Maturity:

http://research.stlouisfed.org/fred2/series/
    DFII10?cid=82

20-Year Treasury Inflation-Indexed Security, Constant Maturity:

http://research.stlouisfed.org/fred2/series/
    DFII20?cid=82

Since the U.S. Treasury changed their extrapolation methodology in December 2008, historical comparison before and after December 2008 isn't as meaningful as otherwise. The charts are updated daily with a few days of lag from the U.S. Treasury data.

Depending on whether you are watching for a specific TIPS issue or the market in general, or whether you want real-time or one-day delayed data, you may find one data source better than another for what you need.

Keep in mind all these prices and yields are for the wholesale market. Prices from a retail broker will be higher due to the dealer's markup.

The question *"Is it a good time to buy TIPS now?"* can only be answered by you. Like the stock market, the bond market is also unpredictable. If you think the yield is good now, it may become better tomorrow. If you think the yield is too low now, it may become even lower.

Some people say the bond market is more efficient than the stock market because there are fewer un-knowns. Whatever you can calculate, the bond dealers can also calculate, except they do it much faster.

Larry Swedroe, financial advisor and author of *The Only Guide to a Winning Bond Strategy You'll Ever Need* and *The Only Guide to Alternative Investments You'll Ever Need*, suggests a shifting strategy in his books. The strategy basically invests more in TIPS and in longer maturities when TIPS yield is high and invests less in TIPS and in shorter maturities when TIPS yield is low.

I agree it's a good time to buy TIPS when the yield goes above 3.0% although I also bought when the yield was lower. It's up to you whether you use Mr. Swedroe's shifting strategy or not.

Another common question about when to buy TIPS is *"Should I buy on the secondary market now or wait for the next auction?"* It's a difficult question to answer because nobody has a crystal ball for what the yield will be when the next auction comes around. Let me give a few points for consideration.

Are the yields on the secondary market very attractive now or just so-so? When you pay a markup on the secondary market, the yield had better be worth it. If it's nothing spectacular, you might as well wait for the next auction.

When is the next auction for the bond you want? Look at the auction schedule (page 62) and see what will be auctioned and when.

If you want a 30-year bond but the upcoming auctions are for 5-year and 10-year, you will have to wait a bit longer for the auction. By that time the good yield may not be available any more.

Or if you want a 15-year bond but they only auction 5-year, 10-year, and 30-year bonds, then you have no choice but to buy on the secondary market.

On the other hand, if you want a 10-year bond and one is coming up for auction next week, it makes sense to wait for the auction because you will get institutional pricing when you buy at auction.

How much more do you pay when you buy on the secondary market? The retail markup is not constant. It varies by time, from broker to broker, and from bond to bond with the same broker. The markup increased dramatically during the market turmoil in 2008. You can use my spreadsheet (URL on page 81) to find out your all-in price and yield including broker commission.

Unfortunately without access to a Bloomberg terminal, there is no good source for real time wholesale market data. You can estimate how much more you are paying over the wholesale prices in a few ways, although none of these methods is perfect.

- Pick a bond that Bloomberg tracks on its web site. Find the retail pricing for that same bond from your broker. Compare the two.
- Compare the current retail price and yield for the bond you want with yesterday's wholesale price and yield as reported by Wall Street Journal.
- Use the average of your broker's bid price and ask price as the proxy for the market price. See how much the ask price is higher than the midpoint between the bid price and the ask price.

Because you pay wholesale pricing when you buy from an auction, the market will have to change that much to your disadvantage for you to be worse off if you wait for the auction.

Let me give a real life example. I was interested in buying a 20-year TIPS in early January 2009. At that time, Fidelity showed the ask price at 127.434 and the ask yield at 2.192% for a TIPS maturing on April 15, 2029.

Because Fidelity doesn't charge commission on top of its markup, I can use the ask price and the ask yield as-is. Wall Street Journal showed as of the previous day's market close, the ask price on the wholesale market for the same bond was 125-17/32, which equals to 125.53125 in decimal, and the ask yield was 2.295%.

So I estimated that if I bought on the secondary market I would pay a markup of

$$127.434 / 125.53125 - 1 = 1.5\%$$

Meanwhile, the auction schedule showed the next auction for a 20-year TIPS was going to be on January 26, 2009, less than a month away.

Because the 2.2% - 2.3% real yield wasn't attractive enough for me to pay a 1.5% markup while the auction was coming up shortly, I decided to wait until the next auction.

Of course when the auction came, the yield could have dropped to below 2.0%. That was the risk I had to take when I made this "buy now or wait" decision.

The actual result from the January 26, 2009 auction came to 2.50%. Waiting for the auction turned out to be the right decision. At other times I've also guessed wrong: buying too soon or holding out for better yield but the market went the other way. It's very difficult to predict what the market will do.

In general I will consider buying on the secondary market if (a) the yield is attractive; and (b) there isn't an auction coming up for the bond I want; and (c) the retail markup is below 0.5%.

Which TIPS?

So you decided this is the time to buy some TIPS on the secondary market. But which one should you buy?

As of February 2010, there are 31 TIPS bonds in the market, with maturities ranging from 2010 to 2040. Much like when you buy a TV you have to decide roughly what size you want, when you buy TIPS, you have to decide what maturity range you want.

A short-term TIPS (less than 5 years till maturity) is less risky. It lets you deploy the money elsewhere if your plan changes, but it protects you against inflation only for a shorter period of time.

A long-term TIPS (greater than 15 years till maturity) is more risky. You are locked in for a long time (this book is primarily focused on buying and holding to maturity, not trading bonds). But a long-term TIPS usually, but not always, has a higher yield. It also gives you inflation protection for a longer period of time.

An intermediate-term TIPS (5-15 years till maturity) is just somewhere in between short-term and long-term.

There are no hard-and-fast rules. You pick the maturity range that suits you.

Of course price and yield matter as well. That's where the yield curve (page 6) comes in.

Fidelity produces a nice yield curve when you look up quotes on its web site. Here's one I got in February 2010:

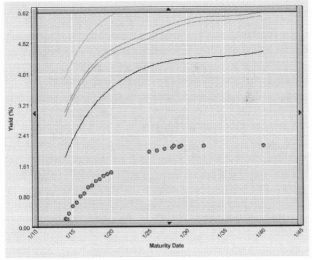

Figure 7: TIPS yield curve, February 2010

Each dot represents a TIPS bond. This chart shows the yield curve was "normal," which means the short-term bonds had lower yields than the longer-term bonds did, whereas when the yield curve is "inverted," it's downward sloped.

By looking at the yield curve and the quote table, I saw the long-term TIPS with 15 years or longer in maturity were yielding 1.9% to 2.1% whereas the shorter term 4- to 10-year TIPS were yielding 0.2% to 1.4%. I don't buy TIPS with less than 3 years in maturity on the secondary market because having inflation protection for only a few years isn't very meaningful to me.

Suppose I decide to buy a TIPS bond in the range of 10 to 20 years, I still have some tough choices to make. For example should I choose a bond maturing in about 10 years yielding 1.433% or a bond maturing in 15 years yielding 1.967%?

I can calculate the so-called *forward rate*, which is the rate I must earn in the remaining 5 years after the 10-year bond matures in order to match the 15-year bond. It's done as follows:

$$\left(\frac{(1 + 1.967\%)^{15}}{(1 + 1.433\%)^{10}} \right)^{\frac{1}{15 - 10}} - 1 = 3.04\%$$

The calculation means that for me to be better off with the 10-year TIPS, 5-year TIPS must yield 3.04% or more ten years down the road. I think that's unlikely. So if I were to choose between these two bonds in February 2010, I would choose the 15-year bond.

I made a spreadsheet that makes the forward rate calculation easier. It's available online at:

http://thefinancebuff.com/go/bond-forward-rate/

If deflation is a concern, you can use the spreadsheet mentioned on page 100 to see how the bonds behave under different inflation and deflation scenarios. I'm not too concerned about deflation more than five years out.

Finally, **don't over-analyze it**. The bond market is efficient. Prices and yields are formed by institutions trading millions of dollars a pop. Whatever calculation we can do with our primitive spreadsheets can be done a thousand times faster by bond traders with their sophisticated computer programs. If you decide to buy a bond on the secondary market, pick one you are comfortable with and go for it.

Where to Buy

You need a brokerage account to buy TIPS on the secondary market. There's no way around it. Treasury-Direct does not sell secondary market TIPS.

If the brokerage firm you use is a small discount broker that does not handle bond orders, you need to find a larger brokerage firm that does. Fidelity, Schwab, E*Trade, TD Ameritrade all do. If you use Vanguard or

T. Rowe Price, you need their brokerage account; a regular mutual fund account is not enough.

If you have accounts with several brokers or if you are buying a large amount, you may be interested in finding out which broker is most cost effective for your order.

Unlike buying stocks, ETFs or mutual funds, commission is only a small part in the cost of buying bonds on the secondary market. The largest cost is the markup included in the quoted price.

The markup is the price difference between what institutions pay for wholesale trades and what your broker charges you for retail purchase. The markup comes from your broker and/or the dealer from which your broker gets the bonds.

A broker that charges you no commission but adds a big markup to the price can be more expensive than a broker that charges you a commission on a smaller markup. Your broker discloses the commission but it never discloses the markup.

Table 13 on the next page lists the commission from a few discount brokers for purchasing TIPS on the secondary market.

Table 13 Commission from Select Brokerage Firms for Buying TIPS on the Secondary Market

Broker	Online Inventory	Commission	
		Online	Broker Assisted
Fidelity	Proprietary	included in markup	$20 + markup
Schwab	Proprietary	included in markup	$25 + markup
E*Trade	BondDesk	included in markup	$20 + markup
Vanguard	BondDesk	$40-$75 + markup	$50-$125 + markup
Zions Direct	BondDesk	$11 + markup	$36 + markup
WellsTrade	BondDesk	no online trading	included in markup

Many brokers use bond price quotes from BondDesk Group. BondDesk is a platform on which some bond dealers post their prices for retail investors. However, two brokers both using BondDesk don't necessarily show the same price for the same bond. Your broker can add a markup to the BondDesk price before showing the price to you. Fidelity and Schwab don't use BondDesk.

Table 14 shows the prices and the total bottom-line costs I got when I priced one particular bond online one day when the market was open. I tried to make them comparable apples-to-apples. I opened multiple browser windows and requested the quotes within a few seconds of each other.

Table 14 Sample Price Quotes

		Total Cost		
	Price	**1 bond**	**10 bonds**	**100 bonds**
Fidelity	97.020	$1,069	$10,694	$106,936
Vanguard	97.293	$1,112 (+$43)	$10,763 (+$69)	$107,309 (+$373)
Zions Direct	97.466	$1,085 (+$16)	$10,767 (+$73)	$107,576 (+$640)
E*Trade	97.830	$1,078 (+$9)	$10,782 (+$88)	$107,821 (+$885)

The numbers in parenthesis are the additional money I would've had to pay if I purchased from a higher cost broker.

Fidelity happened to have the lowest cost for that bond on that day. That doesn't have to be true all the time. Remember these were only for one particular bond on one particular morning. Much like when you buy a TV, this week Sears may sell a Sharp 37" cheaper than Best Buy but Best Buy may sell a Toshiba 52" cheaper than Sears. And next week it could be just the opposite.

You can see the effect of brokerage commission versus markup from this example. Vanguard charges a commission on top of prices from BondDesk whereas E*Trade does not. But in this instance the price from E*Trade was higher. If I bought one bond, Vanguard was more expensive. If I bought 10 bonds or 100 bonds, Vanguard became cheaper than E*Trade.

The lack of pricing transparency on the secondary market is really unfortunate. It makes it difficult for investors to comparison shop.

Most of the online quotes are take-it-or-leave-it. You can't enter a Good-Till-Cancelled limit order and wait for the price to meet what you wanted.

Sometimes the initial online quotes are not even executable. One time I saw a quote from Vanguard but as soon as I tried to place an order to buy, the price went up. But when I tried to place an order to sell, the price went down.

Fidelity lets you enter a limit order within a narrow range. Even those orders are *fill-or-kill* which means if they want to take your price they will do it, otherwise they just throw your order away. If you want to change your limit price you will have to enter a new order.

If you want to get a better price than the online quote, it doesn't hurt to try a limit order below the ask price and slightly above the mid-point between the bid and ask prices. Sometimes it takes a few tries to get the price you want.

grok87, a pseudonym used by a member of an Internet investment forum I frequently visit, suggested entering a limit order at 1/3 of the bid-ask spread Fidelity asks for. People seem to have good success with that.

buy limit price = ask price - (ask price - bid price) / 3

Trading bonds online is still relatively new to brokerage firms. Most of them also offer broker-assisted trades by phone and charge a higher commission.

Is it worth it to place the order by phone? The answer is probably yes, because the phone reps may have access to different systems that provide a better price than what you can get from the online system. This becomes important especially if you are buying a large amount. The price difference can be many times the $25 extra commission for phone orders.

When you talk to the rep by phone, it will be helpful if you know the CUSIP number for the bond you are interested in. CUSIP stands for *Committee on Uniform Security Identification Procedures*. The 9-character alphanumeric CUSIP number uniquely identifies a bond in the same way a ticker symbol does for a stock.

I maintain a spreadsheet with a list of CUSIP numbers of all TIPS bonds on the market. It's available online at:

http://thefinancebuff.com/go/tips-cusip/

Give the CUSIP number to the phone rep and ask for a quote. Compare it with the online quotes from the same broker or a different broker. Challenge the phone rep to give you a better price than the online quote.

Due to the pricing opacity of the secondary market, I only buy on the secondary market when there is really a compelling reason.

Selling

If you don't want to hold your TIPS to maturity, you have to sell it on the secondary market.

Selling is the opposite of buying. A good time to buy TIPS is usually a bad time to sell. Between two TIPS bonds, if one bond looks like a better deal to buy, it's also a worse choice to sell.

When you buy TIPS on the secondary market, you pay a markup above the wholesale price. When you sell TIPS on the secondary market, you pay a markdown below the wholesale price and you receive less for your bonds.

Because of these markups and markdowns, I can only think of two limited cases when it makes sense to sell TIPS on the secondary market:

- Long term TIPS yield is high and you'd like to extend your inflation protection by selling short-term TIPS in order to buy long-term TIPS. You lock in the good yield for more years.

- Long term TIPS yield is low and you'd like to lock in some gains and wait for better opportunities in the future. Please note: the better opportunities may not come any time soon or ever.

In most cases you should just hold your TIPS to maturity.

If you have your TIPS at TreasuryDirect, Treasury-Direct offers a service called *SellDirect*. They ask for quotes from three dealers. They pick the highest bid and then charge you a $45 fee for selling the bonds for you. They won't tell you what the price is before you agree to sell. You will get whatever price they get minus the $45 fee.

If you have your TIPS at a brokerage firm, you will have to ask the bond desk at the broker what the bid price is. Some brokers have an online interface for selling; some don't, and you have to call.

Just like buying TIPS on the secondary market, it's probably a good idea to call instead of taking the price quoted online. The broker on the other side of the line may get you a better price, more than compensating for the higher commission.

Chapter 6 Holding TIPS

Chapters 3 through Chapter 5 are about buying TIPS. For the most part, TIPS are easy to own. You just sit back and collect interest. Either spend the interest or reinvest it. In this chapter you will explore some more details about holding TIPS after your buy them:

- How TIPS are adjusted for inflation
- What happens if there is deflation
- Tax reporting if you own individual TIPS in a taxable account

How TIPS Are Adjusted for Inflation

Both the principal and the interest of TIPS are indexed to inflation. Specifically, the inflation number used is the *Consumer Price Index for All Urban Consumers, Not Seasonally Adjusted* (CPI-U NSA).

This index is calculated by the Bureau of Labor Statistics (BLS), which is a government agency under Department of Labor. Inflation can't be measured in real time. BLS announces the CPI number for the previous month between the 15th and 20th of every month. For example, the CPI numbers for September are announced between October 15th and October 20th.

After the BLS announces the CPI number for the previous month, the Treasury Department applies the difference between the latest CPI number and the previous CPI number to the following month.

For example, suppose on October 15 BLS announces that CPI-U NSA increased by 0.2% in September. The Treasury Department will make the principal value of every TIPS bond go up by 0.2% in November.

The 0.2% increase is applied evenly throughout the month of November. The value will go up a tiny bit every day in November. By the end of November, the inflation in September is fully reflected in the TIPS principal value. As a result, inflation adjustment in TIPS always has a two-month lag.

Every TIPS bond has a Reference CPI number on the date when it was originally issued. The ratio between the current CPI number and the CPI number on the original issue date is called the *index ratio*. The index ratio measures how much CPI-U NSA has changed since the bond was originally issued. The principal value and the interest payments are calculated by the index ratio.

adjusted principal value = $1,000 * index ratio

inflation adjusted price = quoted price * index ratio

interest payment =
    $1,000 * index ratio * interest rate / 2

In nominal dollars, if there is continued inflation, the principal value of a TIPS bond will continue to go up. The interest payments will also continue to go up. If there is a period of deflation, the principal value will go down. So will the interest payments.

In real dollars, both the principal and the interest payments stay the same.

Par Floor. In the rare event when there is net cumulative deflation from the original issue date to the final maturity date, the deflation adjusted principal value will be lower than the face value. If that happens, the U.S. Treasury will pay the face value.

For example, suppose a bond was issued five years ago with a face value of $1,000. Over the five years, deflation has reduced the index ratio to 0.90. When the bond matures, the deflation adjusted principal value becomes $900. Instead of paying the investor $900, U.S. Treasury pays $1,000.

This feature is called the *par floor*. It can be a valuable boost to investors if there is prolonged deflation.

TIPS During Deflation

When you buy TIPS, you are quoted a real Yield to Maturity (YTM). Does the real Yield to Maturity still hold if there is deflation instead of inflation?

During the fourth quarter of 2008, when the stock market was in turmoil, the real yields on TIPS rose sharply. The real yield on 10-year TIPS broke the magic 3% number, a level that hadn't been reached for many years. The concern for deflation was raised as one possible explanation for the rising TIPS yields.

I created a spreadsheet that calculates the effect of deflation on TIPS. The spreadsheet is available online at:

http://thefinancebuff.com/go/tips-deflation

I drew the following conclusions from the spreadsheet exercise:

Conclusion #1: As long as there is cumulative inflation between the date you buy the bond and the date the bond matures, and you hold the bond to maturity, the actual real YTM will match the real YTM quoted at the time of the purchase.

It doesn't matter whether the bond was bought at auction or bought a few years later on the secondary market.

If you buy bonds with a long maturity, say 10 years or more, it's hard to imagine there will be cumulative deflation for that long. Even Japan didn't have deflation for more than a few years. It doesn't matter if there is deflation in some years and inflation in some years, as long as there is net cumulative inflation between the purchase date and the maturity date, the above conclusion holds true.

If you don't believe we will have net deflation lasting a decade or longer, you can skip the rest of the conclusions in this section because they become only academic exercises. Moreover, if we have deflation for that long, there are probably bigger problems to worry about than TIPS yields.

With short maturity TIPS, like 5 years, cumulative deflation is possible.

Conclusion #2: If there is cumulative deflation, there is a chance your real YTM can *increase* but it will never go lower than what you were quoted when you bought the bond.

The possible boost to real YTM comes from the par floor feature in all TIPS (page 102). At maturity, U.S. Treasury will pay the deflation adjusted principal or the face value, whichever is higher.

If there is cumulative deflation between the date the bond was originally issued and the date the bond matures, you will be paid more than the deflation adjusted principal value and therefore your real yield will be higher. Please note the relevant date is the original issuing date, not the date you bought the bond.

Even if there is only deflation after you bought the bond, the bond itself could still experience net inflation during its full lifespan due to inflation between the original issue date and your purchase date. In such case, you will only receive the quoted real YTM, without a bonus.

In nominal terms, you can lose money. In real terms, you can't.

Conclusion #3: All else being equal, a TIPS bond with a lower index ratio at the time of the purchase can receive a higher boost to real YTM during deflation.

The index ratio reflects the net inflation from the original issuing date to the date you buy the bond. A lower index ratio gives you a better chance for a bonus from deflation. However, please note all else are not necessarily equal. The bond market is also aware of the potential bonus. The bond with a lower index ratio can sell at a lower YTM.

Conclusion #4: All else being equal, a TIPS bond with a lower coupon rate can receive a higher boost to real YTM during deflation, although the boost to real YTM is not as sensitive to the coupon rate as to the index ratio.

In short, when you buy a TIPS bond, be confident that your *real* YTM will never go lower than the quote even if there is deflation after you buy the bond. The nominal YTM may be negative during deflation but the real YTM will not be negative unless it was already negative when you bought the bond.

If the real YTM and maturity are comparable between two bonds, first choose the bond with a lower index ratio, then choose the bond with a lower coupon rate, for a better chance for a bonus from deflation.

Finally, remember all these finer points are *moot* unless there is cumulative deflation from the purchase date to the maturity date. If there is no cumulative deflation, all bonds receive the quoted real YTM. One should never say never but it is very unlikely to have cumulative deflation for many years.

Original Issue Discount (OID)

Original Issue Discount (OID) comes into play if you own individual TIPS in a taxable account. It's not an issue if you own individual TIPS in a tax deferred or tax free account. It's also not an issue if you own TIPS mutual funds or ETFs in a taxable account.

Because the U.S. tax system operates on nominal dollars while TIPS work on real dollars, the IRS requires that TIPS investors pay taxes on inflation adjustment to principal every year. The inflation adjustment is treated as an OID.

The IRS publishes rules on OID in Publication 1212 *Guide to Original Issue Discount (OID) Instruments*. You can certainly read the publication for more information, but I think it's easier if I illustrate with a real world example.

Facts. Suppose you bought ten 10-year TIPS (CUSIP 912828GD6) at auction on Jan. 11, 2007. The interest rate was set to 2.375%. The yield was 2.449%. You paid a price of 99.347247 at an index ratio of 0.99995 for an adjusted price of 99.34228 plus $0.06561 per bond as accrued interest on Jan. 16, 2007 (the issue date).

On July 15, 2007, when the bond paid interest, its index ratio was 1.02773. Ten bonds paid interest of

$10,000 * 1.02773 * 2.375% / 2 = $122.04

On Jan. 1, 2008, the index ratio for this TIPS bond became 1.03606. You continue to hold the bonds through 2008. On Jan. 1, 2009, the index ratio for this TIPS bond was 1.07393.

Calculation. You received $122.04 in interest from this TIPS bond. You also paid $0.06561 per bond as accrued interest at the time of purchase. You enter the accrued interest as a negative adjustment on Form 1040 Schedule B *Interest and Ordinary Dividends*, line 1. The net interest income in 2007 was:

$122.04 - $0.06561 * 10 = $121.39

You paid $993.4228 for each $1,000 bond. The *de minimis* rule allows you to treat OID as zero if it's less than 0.25% of the face value times the number of full years until maturity. For this 10-year bond, 0.25% times 10 is 2.5%. A 2.5% discount from $1,000 is $25. Because your discount is only $1,000 - $993.4228 = $6.58 per bond, you can disregard this small discount in the OID calculation.

The inflation adjustment must be treated as OID. The OID due to inflation adjustment between Jan. 16 and Dec. 31, 2007 was:

$$\$10,000 * (1.03606 - 0.99995) = \$361.10$$

This is calculated by subtracting the index ratio on the issue date from the index ratio on January 1 of the following year and then multiplying by $1,000 per bond.

The total interest you report in 2007 was:

$$\$361.10 + \$121.39 = \$482.49$$

You received $122.04 in interest payment from this TIPS but you have to pay tax on $482.49. The difference is also referred to as the *phantom income*.

In 2008, the OID due to inflation adjustment was:

$$\$10,000 * (1.07393 - 1.03606) = \$378.70$$

You add $378.70 to the interest you received in 2008 and report it as the interest income.

If the inflation adjustment OID is negative due to deflation, it offsets against the interest income in the current year and in previous years. If that's not enough, the excess negative OID is carried over to future years.

Your brokerage company is supposed to help you do the math and put the correct OID amount on the 1099-OID form it sends to you. However, if you don't know how to calculate the OID yourself, there is no way for you to verify if they got it right.

If you hold individual TIPS in a taxable account, you have to trust your brokerage firm to do the right calculation and resign to the fact you may end up paying more taxes than you have to, or you'll have to learn how to do the math yourself. Holding TIPS in a tax deferred account or a tax free account, or holding a TIPS mutual fund or ETF will make this math headache go away.

Bond Premium Amortization

Bond premium amortization can also be an issue if you own individual TIPS in a taxable account. It's not an issue if you own individual TIPS in a tax deferred or tax free account. It's also not an issue if you own TIPS mutual funds or ETFs in a taxable account.

Bond premium amortization arises when you buy a bond with a coupon rate above the market yield. The bond pays more interest than you actually earn. The excess is basically a return of the premium you paid. If you amortize the premium, you can reduce the taxes you owe on the interest.

The IRS publishes rules on bond premium amortization in Publication 550 *Investment Income and Expenses* and in regulation 26 CFR 1.171-2. I must admit these are difficult to read or understand. Let me try to illustrate it with a real world example.

Facts. Suppose you bought ten 20-year TIPS (CUSIP 912810FR4) at auction on Jan. 25, 2005. The interest rate was 2.375%. The yield was 2.000%. You paid a price of 106.144524 at an index ratio of 1.01326 for an adjusted price of 107.552 plus $1.06364 per bond as the adjusted accrued interest on Jan. 31, 2005 (the issue date).

Calculation. The first rule about bond premium amortization is you don't have to do it. If you choose not to amortize, you treat the premium you paid as a capital loss when you sell or when the bond matures. This is the simplest way to deal with it.

In 2005, you paid a premium of

$$\$10,000 * (107.552 / 100 - 1.01326) = \$622.60$$

When the bonds mature in 2025, you realize a capital loss of $622.60. If you sell the bonds before they mature, say at an unadjusted price of 103, your capital loss is:

$$\$10,000 * (107.552 - 103 * 1.01326) / 100$$
$$= \$318.62$$

However, it is to your advantage to amortize the premium throughout the life of the bond. This way you pay lower taxes sooner. You use a portion of the premium to reduce the interest income you must report every year.

For TIPS, the bond premium amortization is done as if there is no more inflation or deflation after you purchase the bond.

If there isn't any inflation or deflation after Jan. 31, 2005, your ten TIPS bonds would pay interest twice a year in the amount of:

$$\$10,000 * 1.01326 * 2.375\% / 2 = \$120.32$$

The first interest payment date is July 15, 2005. There are 181 days between the dated date Jan. 15, 2005 and July 15, 2005. There are 165 days between Jan. 31, 2005 (the issue date) and July 15, 2005. Under the constant yield method, the bond would pay interest on July 15, 2005:

$$\$10{,}000 * 1.07552 * 2.000\% / 2 * 165 / 181$$
$$= \$98.04$$

The bond premium amortization on the first interest payment date would be:

$$\$120.32 - \$1.06364 * 10 - \$98.04 = \$11.65$$

Your basis after the bond premium amortization on July 15, 2005 became:

$$\$10{,}000 * 1.07552 - \$11.65 = \$10{,}743.55$$

On the next interest payment date, Jan. 15, 2006, under the constant yield method, the bond would pay interest

$$\$10{,}743.55 * 2.000\% / 2 = \$107.44$$

The bond premium amortization on Jan. 15, 2006 would be:

$$\$120.32 - \$107.44 = \$12.88$$

And your basis on Jan. 15, 2006 became:

$10,743.55 - $12.88 = $10,730.67

You keep doing this for each interest payment until you sell the bonds or until the bonds mature on Jan. 15, 2025. I have an online spreadsheet that shows you how to set up a bond premium amortization schedule. It's available at:

http://thefinancebuff.com/go/tips-premium

Because the bond premium amortization reduces your interest income, you pay less tax on the interest.

You have to decide whether doing the math on bond premium amortization is worth it. Not amortizing is simpler. Putting TIPS in a tax deferred or tax free account or using a TIPS mutual fund or ETF will make this math problem go away.

Market Discount

Like bond premium amortization, market discount is only an issue if you own individual TIPS in a taxable account. It's not an issue if you own individual TIPS in a tax deferred or a tax free account. It's also not an issue if you own TIPS mutual funds or ETFs in a taxable account.

Market discount arises when you buy a bond with a coupon rate below the market yield. The bond pays less interest than you actually earn. When the bond matures, you get a bump in the principal repayment.

The good thing about market discount is that you don't have to account for it every year. Although the IRS allows you to include a small piece of the discount as current interest income while you hold the bond, there isn't a compelling reason for you to do so. You are usually better off deferring the income and the tax.

When you sell the bond or when the bond matures, the market discount is added as interest income, not capital gain.

The IRS publishes rules on market discount bonds in Publication 550 *Investment Income and Expenses*. I illustrate it with a real world example here.

Facts. Suppose you bought ten 10-year TIPS (CUSIP 9128274Y5) at auction on Jan. 6, 1999. The interest rate was 3.875%. The yield was 3.898%. You paid an unadjusted price of 99.811 at an index ratio of 1.00000 for an adjusted price of 99.811 on Jan. 15, 1999 (the issue date).

You held the bond to maturity on Jan. 15, 2009.

Calculation. When you bought the bonds in 1999, you had a discount of

$$\$10,000 * (1.00000 - 99.811 / 100) = \$18.90$$

Therefore you must add $18.90 as interest income when you sell the bonds or when the bonds mature.

Chapter 7 TIPS Strategies

In this concluding chapter I give my recommendation on how to invest in TIPS. There are two parts to the strategies for investing in TIPS:

1. How much of an investor's fixed income investments should be in TIPS versus in nominal bonds; and
2. Whether one should invest in individual TIPS, a TIPS mutual fund, or ETF.

How Much In TIPS

Experts differ in what percentage of fixed income an investor should invest in TIPS. There are several schools of thought on this subject.

TIPS Should Dominate. Proponents of TIPS argue that TIPS should comprise the majority of an investor's fixed income portfolio because the biggest risk in fixed income is inflation and TIPS are guaranteed a real rate of return regardless of actual inflation.

Boston University finance professor Zvi Bodie says TIPS are the safest long-term investment. He sees no point in taking inflation risk with nominal bonds.

Research has also shown that TIPS are a better diversifier to stocks than nominal bonds in a portfolio of both stocks and bonds. TIPS reduce the risk of the overall portfolio more than nominal bonds do.

50:50. Some other experts suggest splitting fixed income investments 50:50 between nominal bonds and TIPS.

Nominal bonds protect against expected inflation and deflation while TIPS protect against unexpected inflation. Nominal bonds have a slightly higher expected return due to the inflation risk premium. Nominal bonds also do better in a financial crisis because of their higher liquidity during "flight to safety."

David Swensen, Chief Investment Officer of Yale Endowment, recommended splitting fixed income investment 50:50 between short-term Treasury bonds and TIPS in his book *Unconventional Success* (ISBN 978-0743228381).

Opportunistic Shifting. Larry Swedroe, investment advisor and author of *The Only Guide to a Winning Bond Strategy You'll Ever Need*, suggested that an investor should shift the fixed income investment between TIPS and nominal bonds and shift the average maturity of TIPS investments based on the real yield and the breakeven inflation rate in the market.

Swedroe suggested investing more in TIPS and lengthening the maturity when the real yield is high or when the breakeven inflation rate is low. Recall from page 26 that the breakeven inflation rate is the difference between the nominal yield and the real yield.

I believe as a general rule TIPS should dominate the fixed income investment. In other words, I invest more in TIPS than I do in nominal bonds. I agree with Professor Bodie that TIPS are the safest long-term investment. When one is investing for safety, taking inflation risk does not make sense.

I also support Larry Swedroe's opportunistic shifting strategy. When real yield is high, I'm glad to lock in a high yield for longer term. When the breakeven inflation rate is low, I invest more in TIPS because there is greater inflation risk in investing in nominal bonds.

TIPS Fund or Individual TIPS

As to the question whether an investor should use a mutual fund or ETF or buy individual TIPS, I believe it's a matter of choice, cost, and convenience.

For retail investors, a TIPS mutual fund or ETF offers a convenient and cost-effective way to invest in TIPS. You get instant diversification, expert management, excellent liquidity, and easy tax reporting.

For ultimate control over maturity and the lowest cost of ownership over the long term, investing in individual TIPS can be better than investing in a TIPS mutual fund or ETF.

Individual TIPS are also an excellent choice for retirees. As each bond in a ladder of individual TIPS matures, the proceeds can be used for income. The average maturity of the TIPS ladder goes down as time goes by, whereas a TIPS mutual fund or ETF does not have a set maturity date.

I invest in both individual TIPS and a TIPS mutual fund. A TIPS mutual fund is an ideal place for reinvesting interest payments from individual TIPS and for accumulating investment until the next auction for the desirable TIPS maturity comes along or when the prices on the secondary market become favorable.

If you are interested in TIPS but you have never invested in them before, I suggest you start with a mutual fund or ETF, then progress to participating in a few TIPS auctions, before you consider buying TIPS on the secondary market. That's how I learned about investing in TIPS. It's also how this book is organized.

Appendix: TIPS Data and Resources

The U.S. government and the news media publish data on TIPS. I also created several spreadsheets to help with the calculations. I mentioned these data sources and tools in this book. Here's a consolidated list of the URLs.

Government Data

U.S. Treasury, *Daily Treasury Real Yield Curve Rates.*

> http://www.treas.gov/offices/domestic-finance/
>   debt-management/interest-rate/real_yield.shtml

U.S. Treasury, *Tentative Auction Schedule*

> http://www.treas.gov/offices/domestic-finance/
>   debt-management/auctions/

U.S. Treasury, *Auction Announcements and Results*

> http://treasurydirect.gov/instit/annceresult/press/
>   press_secannpr.htm

U.S. Treasury, *TIPS/CPI Data*

http://treasurydirect.gov/instit/annceresult/
tipscpi/tipscpi.htm

Federal Reserve Bank of St. Louis, TIPS yield
charts.

*5-Year Treasury Inflation-Indexed Security, Constant
Maturity*

http://research.stlouisfed.org/fred2/series/
DFII5?cid=82

*7-Year Treasury Inflation-Indexed Security, Constant
Maturity*

http://research.stlouisfed.org/fred2/series/
DFII7?cid=82

*10-Year Treasury Inflation-Indexed Security, Constant
Maturity*

http://research.stlouisfed.org/fred2/series/
DFII10?cid=82

*20-Year Treasury Inflation-Indexed Security, Constant
Maturity*

http://research.stlouisfed.org/fred2/series/
    DFII20?cid=82

News Media

Wall Street Journal, *TIPS Market Data.*

http://online.wsj.com/mdc/public/page/
    2_3020-tips.html

Bloomberg, *Government Bonds.*

http://www.bloomberg.com/markets/rates/

My Spreadsheets

I created several spreadsheets for TIPS.

TIPS Auction Schedule

http://thefinancebuff.com/go/tips-auction-schedule/

TIPS auction schedule at a glance. Same as the table on page 62 but I will keep it up to date online as the U.S. Treasury makes changes to the auction schedule.

TIPS Auction Pricing

http://thefinancebuff.com/go/tips-auction-spreadsheet/

This spreadsheet estimates the all-in cost for TIPS purchased at auction.

TIPS CUSIP List

http://thefinancebuff.com/go/tips-cusip/

A list of all TIPS bonds on the market.

Bond Forward Rate

http://thefinancebuff.com/go/bond-forward-rate/

This spreadsheet calculates the forward rate. It helps decide on which issue to buy.

Buying TIPS on Secondary Market

http://thefinancebuff.com/go/tips-secondary-market/

This spreadsheet calculates the all-in cost and yield for TIPS purchased on the secondary market.

TIPS During Deflation

Appendix

http://thefinancebuff.com/go/tips-deflation/

This spreadsheet shows the effect of deflation on TIPS.

TIPS Premium Amortization

http://thefinancebuff.com/go/tips-premium/

This spreadsheet gives an example for how to amortize the bond premium for tax purposes.

About the Author

The Finance Buff a.k.a. TFB is a pseudonym used by a blogger who writes a blog by the same name at *thefinancebuff.com*.

TFB holds an MBA degree in Finance. He also has a Certified Employee Benefits Specialist (CEBS) designation from the International Foundation of Employee Benefit Plans and the Wharton School of Business, University of Pennsylvania.

TFB has been sharing his experience and thoughts about personal finance with online readers since 2006. Today, more than 50,000 people visit his blog in any month. He was the author of a chapter on defined benefit pension plans in *Bogleheads' Guide to Retirement Planning* (John Wiley & Sons, 2009).

In his copious spare time, TFB enjoys hiking.

Index

Made in the USA
Lexington, KY
10 April 2010